Streetwise

Isabel Wright worked for Women's Aid (the organisation which helps battered women) in Leicester and
London, and in 1978 decided to take up karate 'so that I
could defend myself and not feel frightened when on
my own'. She then worked with other women in her
karate group to develop a self-defence approach particularly geared to women's needs. She is now involved
in training more women to teach this approach as well
as being active in both the London and national network
of women's self-defence teachers.

Judith Lowe is an actress and writer who has worked
with various children's and community theatre groups
and has also appeared in several TV productions. Her
interest in karate led her to become involved in women's
self-defence generally and she is an original member of
the London Women's Self-defence Teachers' Group.
She now helps to train self-defence teachers and took
part in the making of the BBC TV series *Streetwise*.

Michael Finn is an expert in martial arts with black
belts in Judo, Kendo and Aikido, amongst others. As an
officer with the City of London police he instructed col-
leagues from his own and other forces in the art of self-
defence and also lectures to school-children. He now
runs his own martial arts training school and has written
several books on the subject.

STREET WISE

A basic guide to self-defence

Judith Lowe

Isabel Wright

Michael Finn

Edited by Jenny Rogers

ARIEL BOOKS
BRITISH BROADCASTING CORPORATION

© The contributors 1984
First published 1984

Published by the British Broadcasting Corporation
35 Marylebone High Street, London W1M 4AA

Typeset by Phoenix Photosetting, Chatham
Printed in England by Mackays of Chatham Ltd
Cover printed by Belmont Press Ltd, Northampton

Set in 10/12 point Linotron Ehrhardt

ISBN 0 563 21057 5

Contents

Introduction

This book is intended to give you some simple, basic advice on how to cope with difficult and dangerous situations on the street or at home. It is aimed at people of all ages and abilities; it is also aimed at both men and women.

It deals with questions like: Is it best to give in or to fight back? Can ordinary, unfit people really learn to defend themselves? What can you do to make your home secure? How should you behave if you discover a burglar in your house? What can you tell children that will protect them from possible attack?

Unlike many other books on self-defence, learning 'moves' forms only a small part of this book. Instead, we concentrate on the simple precautions that any of us can take in daily life and also on developing a strong, confident frame of mind – a vital part of self-defence.

It is important to say that this book is only meant as an introduction to a complex subject. To learn more, you will need to join a self-defence class.

What is self-defence?
It may surprise you to learn that self-defence is not a 'martial art'. Self-defence, by our definition, includes any common-sense technique which helps you look after yourself. Most people have been practising self-defence all their lives. For instance:

I always carry my keys in my hand so that I can get quickly into my house without fumbling in my pocket on the doorstep.

I always sit in a railway carriage where there are plenty of other people about.

I've put some good locks on my doors and windows. I always ask someone to identify themselves before I open the door.

I've been in a situation with someone who was threatening to kill me. I managed to talk them out of hurting me.

Someone snatched my purse. I grabbed their wrist and shouted, 'Give it back'. They were so surprised that they did.

If I go out to a party I always arrange to get a lift back with another woman.

My boss kept on making sexual remarks about me. I went into his office and told him to stop doing it.

All these people were using self-defence. They had thought of ways to feel safer and more in control of potentially dangerous situations. Self-defence does not just mean fighting. It also includes joking your way out of danger, bluffing, lying, shouting and using distraction. Many versions of these strategies are suggested and recounted in this book and you will, no doubt, be able to think of more yourself.

There are no rules or foolproof techniques. What works for one person may not work for another: what has worked for you in one situation may not be right in another apparently similar one. Good self-defence means trusting your intuitions and then having the courage to act on them. It is also about self-confidence. The greater your confidence, the greater your freedom to choose the best response.

Some people claim that self-defence can only be practised by the young and fit. This is not true. Some of the best self-defence stories we have collected have come from elderly people who were not physically strong. For instance, a man of 72 was attacked on the street one winter night. His booming 'shout', developed through years as a 'tic tac' man on a race course, was enough to send his astonished and then frightened attacker running off. A disabled 74-year-old woman was pinned to the wall by a young man who demanded her rings and her money. Furiously angry, she somehow wrested one arm free and shook her walking stick over his head, shouting, 'I'll crack your skull if you don't leave me alone'. He ran off empty-handed.

Many of the physical techniques we have given in this book have been specially developed so that they can be learnt and used by people with little muscular strength. Everyone should be able to find something they can do.

Perhaps the biggest single worry which many people have about self-defence is that by defending yourself you might make matters worse. This is a difficult question, but all the best self-defence involves making an individual choice based on your assessment of the situation at the time which might well be to fight back.

In general, many attackers expect you to behave like a 'victim' – to cower, to be frightened, to beg and to plead. As you begin to think about self-defence and to practise it, you will become more confident. This confidence will communicate itself to people around you and might in itself help to deter an attacker. If dangerous situations do arise, a confident manner may also help you to cope, as this man discovered:

> I was 40 when this happened a few years ago and was, even then, very seriously disabled by arthritis. I walked only with great difficulty using a stick. I also had one built-up shoe. One day I got into a difficult argument with a neighbour who was perhaps five years younger and always looked very fit. He became very angry and put his hands tightly round my neck as if he was going to strangle me. He shouted, 'God is good, you are a cripple and I will kill you'. I looked him steadily in the eye, though inwardly I felt very frightened, and simply said, 'I'm telling you now – don't do that, take your hands away'. He withdrew his hands and shuffled off indoors looking more than a little foolish.

Learning some simple self-defence will mean that you *can* look after yourself. It will give you confidence and, by doing so, will also considerably reduce your chances of being attacked in the first place.

How other people have coped

Hearing about how other people defended themselves is always encouraging, even though people often do not see what they do as 'proper' self-defence unless they actually hit their attacker. But such stories can also leave you asking yourself if you could ever be equally inspired under stress. Remember that people take these actions without consciously thinking of the 'cleverest' strategies to adopt. They simply 'read' the situation and act.

Remember, too, that you may not realise at the time that your tactics will work. When a course of action does prevent a serious attack the tactic itself can almost become invisible:

> I always look to see who is around when I go into my block of flats. Quite often there are gangs of teenage boys hanging about. Several women have been robbed and their empty bags get dumped at the bottom of the stairs later on. One day when I went in, there didn't seem to be anyone around. I started walking up the stairs when suddenly I felt I needed to turn round. I hadn't heard or felt anything in particular, but I felt uneasy. I turned round and there was a boy of about 18 standing right behind me. I looked him in the eyes and all I thought was how blue his eyes were. I turned back and went on up the stairs. It was only much later that I realised he must have been about to jump me. Why else would he stand so close and silently behind me? I can't say how I knew that I should turn round. I didn't think about what to do, I just did something and moved on. Maybe nothing would have happened anyway, I can never know that. All I know is that I did what came instinctively and didn't get hurt. That's enough for me!

When you read the stories in this book, don't see them as illustrating the 'best' solution and be left wondering, 'Could I have done that?' They only show one person's resourcefulness. Also, almost all the people describing their experiences have said: 'I amazed myself – I wouldn't have thought I could be so brave'.

You may find that if you think back over your own encounters you are not sure how successfully you defended yourself. Remember that the aim of self-defence is to come away as unscathed as possible – is that what happened to you? 'As unscathed as possible' may mean that you were hurt, but *could* have been hurt much more.

Further reading

BROWNMILLER, Susan *Against our will* Penguin Books, 1975

DICKSON, Anne *A woman in your own right* Quartet Books, 1982

HASLER, Gordon *Protect your property and defend yourself* Penguin Books, 1982

NELSON, Sarah *Incest: fact and myth* Stramullion, 1982

QUINN, Kaleghl *Stand your ground* Orbis Publishing, 1982

Thinking ahead

Trusting your intuition

Trusting your instinct that something is 'wrong' is a vital first step in self-defence, as it often enables you to escape from trouble before it has really started:

> I was on my own when I heard someone on the stairs in my house, which was divided into flats. It was dark and he hadn't put the lights on, that was the first thing, so obviously he didn't know the house. Feeling slightly foolish (but I knew something was wrong) I said, 'Who are you?' He said he was a minicab driver and had come for the people in the top flat. He began to look uneasy and said he'd wait outside. I followed him downstairs, and he sat on the bonnet of a car there, raising his eyes to heaven as if to say 'Why on earth are they so long?' I closed the front door. Five minutes later I looked out again, and the car was still there but he had vanished!

Intuition often seems illogical and appears to have a 'magical' quality because it is so hard to pin down. In fact, it is developed out of years of intricate and accurate observation of other people's behaviour. An intuitive judgement is made so quickly that it is only later possible to begin analysing it.

It might look at first as if you were being 'irrational' or just 'lucky' to have been able to pick up so clearly what was about to happen. Most people have had experiences where they acted on a vague sense that something was wrong and have found later that their instinct was correct:

> There was a man at my door and he said he was from the gas board. He had an identification with him, but I still didn't feel right about letting him into my house. There was something wrong with my gas cooker and I had 'phoned for them to come round. I don't know what it was about him. He just gave me the creeps somehow! Anyway I wouldn't let him in though he was very persuasive. He kept on saying it would cost me money if he had to come out again. I said I'd phone

the gas board while he waited on the doorstep. When I did they said they had no record of his call. When I went back to the door he'd gone.

Many times people who have suffered an attack will say, 'I knew there was something wrong, but I just thought I was being stupid so I pretended that everything was all right – and it wasn't'. But intuition must be trusted. One way to develop it is to start *intercepting* all those messages which say 'I'm stupid' or 'I can't' and replacing them with positive messages which say 'I'm right, I *can* do something'.

One woman in a self-defence class said 'I call intuition being careful'. Intuition *is* a form of carefulness, an alertness to all the tiniest details of an encounter and a capacity to co-ordinate these details in a rapid and open way.

The women who did not believe their 'gasman' or 'minicab' callers had taken in many objective facts about them, which they may not even have fully realised at the time. The woman who encountered the bogus gasman had probably noticed his face, the kind of eye contact he was making with her, his whole 'body language', his use of words, his clothes and other details which added up to a feeling that the man might not be genuine. She felt anxious but trusted herself enough to listen to her anxiety and to act on it.

Intuition is about awareness, it is about trusting the validity of your own observations and being prepared to act on them even if this means making an 'embarrassing' public challenge.

Intuition works best when you are standing strongly and breathing correctly, so in the following sections we give you some basic exercises to develop calmness and alertness.

Standing strong

Knowing that you stand firmly will help you prepare yourself positively against a possible attack.

Fright makes you physically less stable and affects your state of mind. To face an attacker, and to be able to think and act clearly, it is important to have your feet firmly planted on the ground. Once you know how to do this it will help you to face everyday situations from a firmer base too.

Disabled people may find it uncomfortable to stand with their

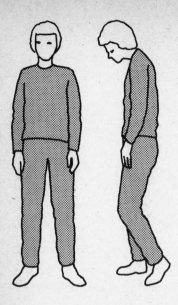

Standing strong (left) will help you face an attacker confidently. Looking unconfident (right) may make you seem more vulnerable.

weight equally balanced over both feet. They should try to find the most comfortable and stable position. One woman with multiple sclerosis said:

> I know I can't be stable on my feet. But I feel fine on the ground. And I know how to fall without hurting myself because I do it all the time. If I were attacked I would probably try and defend myself from sitting on a chair or lying or sitting on the ground. That is the safest, strongest place for me to be.

Think about how you normally stand. Is it with most weight on one leg or leaning into one hip, or with your feet crossed over each other?

Now stand with your feet hip-width apart and facing straight forward.

Rock gently forwards and backwards, gradually decreasing the rocking until you can feel your weight evenly poised between the heel and the ball of the foot. Now do the same again, but this time rocking from side to side, aiming to finish with the weight balanced on both feet.

Bend your knees very slightly to lower your weight.

The top of your body should be loose and flexible, and able to move without resistance if someone pulls or pushes you. Get a friend to try this and see whether your top half is stiff or flexible.

Your legs and hips should be solid and 'grounded' but ready to take a step in any direction should you be pulled or pushed hard. Imagine you are a tall tree with long roots going deep into the ground.

Practise standing or sitting so that you feel really stable whenever you can, but especially when you feel tense. When people are anxious or frightened they tend to tense their muscles upwards. Whether you stand or sit or lie, you are stronger and more free to move and to *think clearly* if you can let go of that tension. Make your shoulders relax and let your weight sink down towards the floor to make you stable and heavy.

Breathing

Breathing is something that is taken for granted but it deserves proper attention. Good breathing uses the whole of the lungs, supplying oxygen to the body and clearing the system of waste. Good breathing ought to come naturally, but because of our tense and sedentary lives many people do not breathe fully. This means that minds and bodies are not able to work efficiently. When surprised or frightened, people often hold their breath: 'It quite took my breath away' is a physical as well as emotional reaction. Depriving the muscles of oxygen by irregular breathing handicaps the body's capacity to operate efficiently. Controlled breathing is essential to cope with panic in an attack.

To restore calm breathing you must breathe correctly – from the *diaphragm*. This is a muscle between waist and lungs; it is one of the strongest muscles in the body. If you are breathing correctly, your shoulders will not rise when your lungs fill.

Try an experiment: place your hands over your diaphragm, fingertips touching. Take a deep breath. If you are using your diaphragm correctly, the fingertips should be forced apart by the movement of the diaphragm and your shoulders will not rise. If this does not happen, try taking different types of breaths until you get the right one.

Breathing exercises will help improve your general well-being:

- Lie down. Take some normal breaths.
- Count your breathing to establish a rhythm: 'In – 2 – 3, out – 2 – 3'. After a few breaths lengthen the count so that you are breathing 'In – 2 – 3 – 4, out – 2 – 3 – 4'. Lengthen the breath by

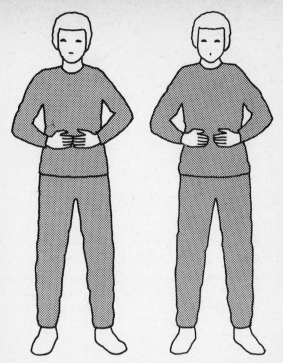

Correct breathing. Your finger tips start by touching (left). They should be forced apart (right) when you breathe in.

one count after each 5–10 breaths until you are counting to 5, 6 or 7, whichever is comfortable. Don't strain. Let the breath flow in and out freely. The 'out' breath is especially important since a long slow out-breath calms the whole body.

● Be aware of using your whole lungs. Can you feel them working from the bottom? Are they expanding sideways into your ribs? Your shoulders should stay down and relaxed while your lungs expand sideways and downwards.

● Go back to normal breathing for a couple of minutes before standing up. Stand up slowly so that you don't feel dizzy.

● Repeat the same sequence standing or sitting up. Stand or sit in a relaxed way. Let your chest be as open as possible without straining, as it was when it was supported by the floor. Be aware that your lungs and ribs are expanding sideways, and that your shoulders do not rise with each breath.

● Now practise some deep relaxed breathing. Use your breathing *in* to take in strength and energy, and your breathing *out* to send that strength around your body, into your pelvis and legs and feet and into your 'roots'. Continue this for several minutes.

When you find yourself in a dangerous situation, you should be able to use regular diaphragmatic breathing to calm yourself down.

You may feel that you have no problem becoming angry and expressing violent emotions, but are worried that your anger would be too powerful. You may be frightened that you could do more damage in a fight than you mean to.

It is important that you feel you have real choices about your responses to danger, and that you are not frightened of your own capacity to be violent. Feeling out of control – either through being paralysed with fear, or through being wild with anger – does not make you feel safe. Standing strong and breathing correctly will help you cope with panic and strong feelings of fright or anger. This way you will think more clearly in an emergency.

Voice

Learning to shout was the most exciting thing for me! Before, if I yelled I would hurt my throat and the sound came out all tight and strangled. When I shouted loudly it sounded desperate rather than strong. Now when I shout I can feel my feet firmly on the ground, my lungs working freely and my throat open. I put the whole of myself into that sound.

Your voice is a basic weapon in self-defence. Using your voice has several advantages.

First, it makes you breathe. Fright or panic may make you hold your breath. Remembering to shout will start you breathing deeply.

Secondly, your voice gives a message to your attacker and to yourself, irrespective of the words you use. He will expect silence, or a scream, a sound full of fear and panic. Give him a yell full of strength and confidence and he will be startled. You will both begin to realise just who he is up against:

I was buying a magazine at a busy station bookstall when I felt a man suddenly lurch into me. I looked round annoyed but he'd made off.

Then I saw him sneak off and do the same to another woman, then another – this time a frail-looking woman with a stick. I was furious. I marched up to him and shouted: 'You are a pest, push off or I'll fetch the police', in an extremely loud voice. About 30 people on the concourse stopped and stared. He went bright red and ran off.

Shouting as you move strengthens any action you make, because it lets you breathe effectively and puts more force and conviction into your movements. Practise shouting and breathing as you punch and kick.

Shouting may also serve to call for help or attract the attention of the people around.

I had just got out of a taxi late one night when a young chap about 17 appeared out of nowhere and demanded my money – right outside my own front door! I said extremely loudly: 'Go and get your mother to tuck you up in bed, sonny, otherwise I shall SMACK YOUR BOTTOM FOR HER'. I really yelled the last bit. Someone over the road flung up a window. He'd gone before they'd even got their head out.

Many people, but especially women, find it hard at first to use their voices freely and strongly. Women have been told over and over again that it is not feminine to make a lot of noise. It is also generally considered unfeminine for women to have deep voices and so, by holding tension in their throats, many women have voices several tones higher than if their throats' were relaxed. In extreme panic people's throats may become so tense that they cannot utter a sound. So it is important to learn to relax the throat and let out sounds that are deep and powerful. This is the purpose of the 'ki' or yell used in martial arts – to release the energy and spirit behind the actions. Here are some hints on relaxing and strengthening the voice.

● Repeat the breathing exercise sitting or standing, but this time let out sound as you breathe out. This can start as a murmur or a sigh. Gradually make it louder until it is as loud as it can go without feeling as though you are straining. With practice you will be able to make a louder noise without hurting your throat.

● Imagine your breath carrying the sound coming from deep down in your lungs and travelling up through an open relaxed throat. Open your mouth widely enough to let the sound escape freely.

● Whenever you use your voice for talking, singing or shouting, try to keep it relaxed. Feel when your throat becomes tense, and breathe into it to relax it. Does your voice get higher when you get tense? Consciously try to bring it down lower so that you sound strong and convincing.

Body language

It is often easy to see how someone is feeling simply by how they express themselves with their body. This has come to be known as 'body language'. When you are depressed you may sit still and slumped; when you are happy your body and voice take on lightness and energy. Fear makes people tense – your shoulders rise, your face looks withdrawn, your fists clench and your breathing becomes fast, irregular and shallow. And there are subtler messages too – a slight change of colouring, a tremor, a hesitation. Everyday we 'read' people's moods from the messages they give out physically. Faced with an attacker you will do the same. And he will 'read' you from your physical reactions.

There are two ways in which body language will help you. First, you can become more aware of other people's body language; notice how people sit and stand, their hands, faces, voices; see what you learn about them from what you see and how that affects your reaction to them.

Secondly, notice your own body language and what messages you generally give to people about who you are. Are these the messages you want to give, or would you like to find ways of showing different sides of yourself?

> When I'm nervous, for instance meeting new people, I get quite aggressive to cover up how shy I feel. I talk a lot and stand much closer to them than I normally would. Then, if they back off I feel even worse. The other day when I met someone for the first time I tried to be different. I stood much further back, took deep breaths and made myself talk slowly. It was so difficult! But I couldn't believe how different it felt. The man I was talking to actually came slightly towards me, which made me feel he really wanted to be talking to me.

Learning to express a confident feeling with your body may also be an important way to deter an attacker. A manner which communicates 'I am confident, I am alert, I am not a victim' may be the best possible deterrent to someone looking for an easy target.

Assertion

An important aspect of self-defence is believing in your own value as a person enough to want to defend yourself:

> I was outside a bicycle shop with my bike because I was going to buy a basket. My wallet was on the ground nearby as I locked my bike. Suddenly I noticed that a man had taken my wallet and was putting it into his pocket. I said, 'Give me back my wallet' and, after a struggle, snatched it back from him. I'd always thought I'd be terrified in a situation like this but amazingly I just felt colossally angry. Why should he have my money? I'd worked hard for it. I didn't deserve to have it stolen from me.

But some people find that asserting themselves does not come easily. They may agree to do things they resent, they may appear pleasant and friendly when underneath there is anger. They may fail to ask for what they want for fear of appearing demanding. In all this behaviour there is a common theme: 'What I feel or want is not important. I am not important.'

The causes of this behaviour are too complex for this book, though some of these attitudes clearly arise from society in general and the way people are treated unequally because of their age, gender, physical abilities, race and social class.

To defend yourself, you must assert yourself – *you do not deserve to be attacked*.

> I was followed in the street by a man who made insulting sexual suggestions. He kept walking with me in spite of the fact that I was ignoring him. I was so angry that he should treat me like that that I stopped and turned round to face him. I told him exactly what I thought of him in terms which I won't repeat to you. He was completely astonished. His whole expression changed and he looked really weak. I then carried on walking. I felt very shaken and upset and I was trembling for several hours afterwards. But I felt very pleased with myself. It was the first time I had ever done anything like that.

This woman rejected the man's image of her as an object to be abused and humiliated. She asserted her own dignity and humanity. She knew that she did not deserve to be treated in such an insulting way.

If you are not an assertive person, you may need to begin by changing your attitudes to yourself. Next time you fail to ask for what you want, think how you felt and why you gave in. Then imagine behaving differently. What would you like to have said? How would you say it? How do you think other people would react to you?

In everyday life being assertive should mean being sensitive to other people's needs as well as your own. However, in self-defence, it does mean putting your own needs first.

Press-ups

Learning the correct way to do press-ups can be a valuable way of practising assertion.

Press-ups use the powerful muscles across the chest and arms. They are the muscles with which we embrace the people in our life whom we want close to us – we say 'YES' with these muscles. We also use them to say 'NO' and push away what we do not want. So it is particularly important to develop strength in this area.

In a press-up it is the arms that do the 'work' of bending and bearing most of the weight. The back should be kept straight. Do not let your bottom dip up and down while your arms remain stiff.

Keep the body light and free from tension. Feel that you connect openly to the strength in your back, so that although it is straight, it does not feel rigid and closed off from your arms and chest.

It is easy to find that you are putting most of the effort of your press-ups into a clenched jaw and neck! Think of the neck being free from tension, the shoulders dropped and open, the spine long and straight. Think of the chest widening and opening from the heart.

Keep this feeling of lightness and use your breathing to give you assertiveness.

Breathe *in* on the way down and *out* on the way up. Remember that you do not have to go all the way down – just so long as your arms are free from tension and the elbows are doing the outward bending.

If you want to, practise against a wall to begin with, or practise from a kneeling position, still keeping the back straight and your bottom in line with your back.

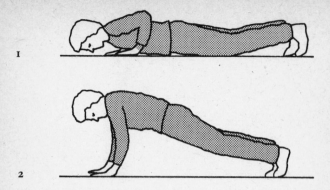

(1) Lie flat on your stomach. Place the hands on the floor under the shoulders. Breathe in. (2) Push up, breathing out or counting – straighten the arms.

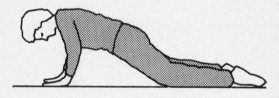

Alternatively you can do press-ups from a kneeling position. Remember to keep the back straight. You don't have to go all the way down, just so long as you are exercising the arms.

Use the push upwards to shout if you want to. Anything you do in the way of a punch or kick is stronger when you put your breath and your voice behind it.

You can shout 'YES!' or 'NO!' and see how each of them feels. Or you could shout 'I WILL!' or 'I WON'T!' or any other assertive message. For example, breathing in to go down, come up shouting 'I'M MAUREEN!' (or whoever), breathe in to go down, come up shouting 'I'M STRONG!'

Fighting

Many men and women dislike the idea of having to defend themselves with physical force. Many think themselves incapable of fighting, either because of what they imagine to be their temperament – 'I'm just a coward', or their physique – 'I'm not fit'. Many simply shrink from the idea of hurting others.

Much of this book concentrates on forms of self-defence other than fighting, but we do also look at simple physical techniques and moves. Fighting is one option among many available to you in self-defence. You will choose it if it seems to be the most appropriate response. You may see it as something to fall back on if other tactics do not stop the situation getting out of hand. At times it may be your first or only possible response to an attack.

You may have been in a physical fight and know exactly what to do. But many people, especially women, do not know how to fight because it is something they have never learnt or been allowed to learn. We all absorb the idea that 'girls don't fight' or that when girls do, 'all they can do is pull hair, bite and scratch'. These can be useful tactics, but so can a strong well-aimed punch or kick, especially in more serious situations.

Women have also grown up learning that it is their job to nurture, nurse and protect people from pain. When the dread of hurting someone is so deeply instilled, this may make it hard for a woman to fight, even to save her own life. It also means that women often feel guilty or ashamed if they do hurt someone in self-defence.

Many men also dislike the idea of hurting someone, so it is valuable for both sexes to look at feelings about fighting, at the same time as learning the physical techniques. Look at the diagram of the vulnerable areas of the body. Imagine how you would set out to hurt each area – with a punch? a poke? a kick?

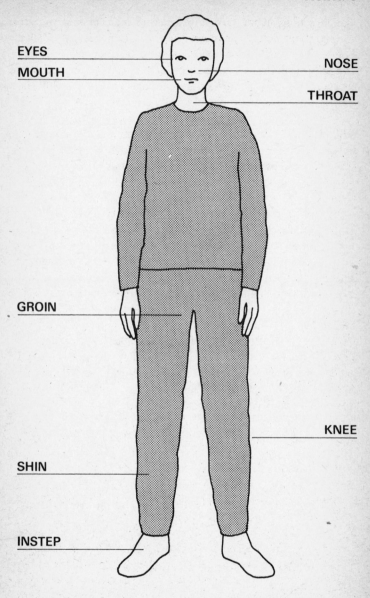

EYES

MOUTH

NOSE

THROAT

GROIN

KNEE

SHIN

INSTEP

It is useful to know which are the most vulnerable parts of the body in case you do have to defend yourself against an attacker.

Which actions might serve to warn your attacker that you are serious about defending yourself? Which actions might break a limb? Which might cause permanent damage? Which ones can you imagine doing and in what sort of situation? Remember that there are no 'right' moves for particular situations, only the moves which you feel you could do, and do with conviction.

Remember, too, that you are doing these things in self-defence, which is very different from imagining how you could *attack* anyone in these ways. Recognise that in an attack someone intends to hurt you, maybe seriously, and that you may have to hurt back in order to stop them.

If you are in a situation where you need to fight, it is important to do it with conviction. If you are half-hearted, you may just anger your attacker and give both of you the feeling that you cannot fight properly. So in a fight you must summon up all your energy, your courage, your desire to protect yourself and fight as though you really mean it.

Even if you do fight off your attacker you may have mixed feelings about it afterwards. On the one hand you will be glad that you were strong and brave enough to send him off, but at the same time you may feel shocked and upset at having been attacked and at having hurt someone. All these feelings are real and need taking care of. It is important to remember that you were strong and effective. It is also important to value your reluctance to hurt someone as it shows your regard for human life.

How to practise
If you are going to take self-defence seriously, you will need to practise some 'fighting' techniques with someone you trust.

It is important to set up your practice sessions carefully, otherwise you could find yourself demoralised and disheartened. For instance, some women learn a few techniques and then say, 'I tried this on my husband and it didn't work. I'm not as strong as he is'. When she describes what happened it usually turns out that her husband (or boyfriend or brother) grabbed her as hard as he could. She was naturally unwilling to fight back as hard as she could for fear of hurting someone she loved. It was obviously inappropriate to knee him in the groin, or jab him in the eye. It was not an attack. But what has happened is that a completely unfair bargain has been made. Her partner is using all his strength to hold on to her, but she is not able to use all of hers to escape in case she hurts him. There is no real danger, so the other skills which she might have used, like talking her way out of the situation, or distracting him in some way, cannot work for her. She is left believing that there is nothing she can do. The real danger in practising like this, is that confidence can be undermined.

Don't practise with someone if you suspect that their only interest is to prove how weak you are in comparison to them.

A lot of people feel insecure or frightened of their physical strength, so work slowly and carefully. For example, if you are practising getting out of the holds from behind, you could start with the 'attacker' simply standing behind you while you practise the different techniques you could use. Next, they could hold you very lightly while you work through all the possibilities and find out which ones suit you best.

Later, you can add other physical techniques such as 'standing strong', breathing regularly, or shouting. You may want to think about a particular situation like 'What can I do if someone grabs my wrist and won't let go?' but try to avoid the temptation of adding to the problem before you have fully explored the one you have set yourself. For instance, when you are halfway through, don't suddenly say to yourself, 'But what if there were three of them, and they all had knives?'

Self-defence will develop your confidence and your own sense of self-worth, and you are entitled to ask your partner to let go of you to stop a particular exercise, if it does not feel right for you. Learn to trust your own judgement here.

When you are practising the different fighting techniques, it is a good idea to observe your own feelings. Do you feel lethargic or half-hearted? Or are you wild and out of control? Try to notice if you tend to hold back your punch or if your aim is wild, or if your strikes lose their strength at the last minute.

And remember, self-defence works! With some techniques, such as escaping from grabs, you will only make each other's wrists sore by practising strongly. But if you punch someone on the nose, even in practice, you will hurt them. So where there is any risk of causing real damage, stand far enough away to avoid hurting each other.

Also, it is important to remember that practice is totally different from a real attack. Practice prepares you by giving you skill and confidence, but it cannot simulate the emotions and conditions of a real attack.

In a real attack, for example, you can assess what the motive for the attack might be; you can assess what sort of person the attacker is and his emotional state. Also, you can assess the difference made by the environment: for instance, whether you could run away or call for help. You react to a whole situation and combine whatever verbal and physical skills you feel will be most effective for that particular occasion. Your senses are sharpened and your mind races through all the possible courses of action. Fear and anger also have profound physical effects. Adrenalin rushes round your body adding strength and increasing stamina. In dangerous situations your will to survive beats as strongly as your heart. Your whole range of skills and your most powerful feelings combine to give you effectiveness and strength.

Strikes to vulnerable areas

You may have to defend yourself by striking back. Here are some suggestions for techniques which involve strikes with the hand.

When you are practising the moves remember to stop short of the target. In a real attack, however, you would need to 'strike through' the target, that is to have the intention of hitting beyond the target. Some of the strikes involve making a fist. It is important to do this correctly as otherwise you could break your fingers.

Curl up your fingers, then tuck the curled fingers tightly into the palm. Bend your thumb to bind the index and middle fingers – you should barely be able to see your fingernails. The fist should be compact but not tense.

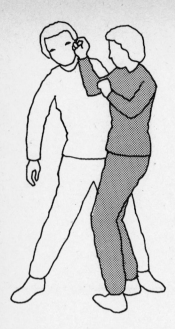

A hammer blow with the side of the fist to the temple.

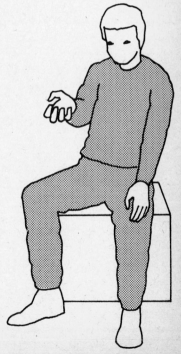

It is possible to make a strike even from a sitting position. This shows the defender preparing to grab, twist and pull the attacker's testicles. 'Grab, twist and pull' is a useful general principle to apply to other soft, fleshy parts of the attacker's body.

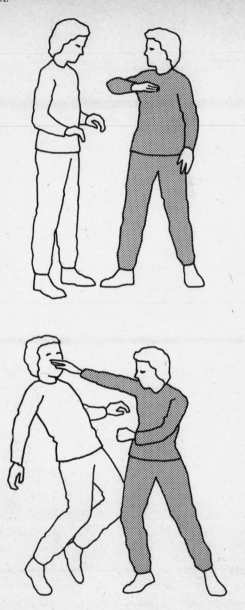

A strike with the knife edge part of the hand underneath the attacker's nose.

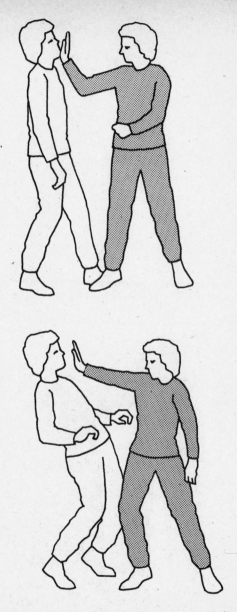

A strike with the heel of the hand underneath the attacker's chin.

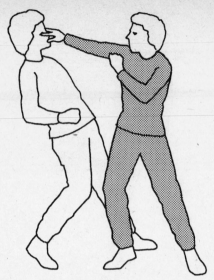

A poke to the eye, keeping the fingers stiff.

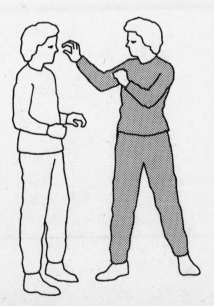

A claw to the face – the attacker's cheeks would be scratched.

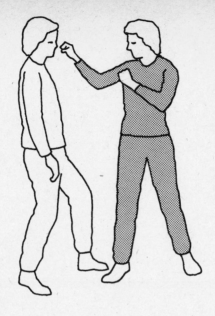

Punch to the attacker's nose – remember to keep the fist straight.

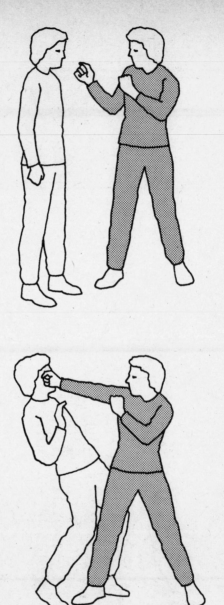

Knuckle to the eye – make a fist with the first joint of the middle finger protruding.

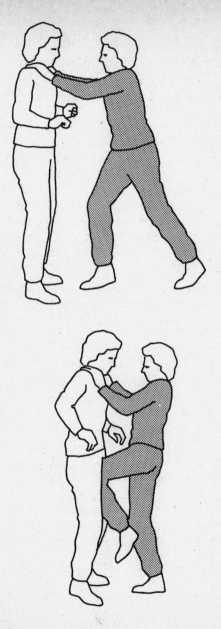

Knee to the groin – support yourself by holding onto the attacker. Bring the knee up sharply, well between the legs.

Classes

This book is only intended as an introduction to a complex subject. If you want to take it further, then you could enrol for a self-defence class. Some enlightened employers and schools now run self-defence courses, but the majority are organised by Adult Education Institutes or sports centres. Unfortunately, classes exist only patchily throughout Great Britain and vary tremendously in quality. A good class will have a sympathetic and sensitive teacher who will make you feel welcome whatever your age, sex, race, or state of fitness. Always try to visit a class first, before committing yourself to it.

When choosing a class think about who you want to learn with. For example, you may wish to be part of a women-only group so that you can share your experiences. This might be particularly important if you want to discuss rape and sexual harrassment: a group of women will know how you feel. Black or Asian women may prefer to work with other black or Asian women who understand the problems created by racism. Physically disabled or elderly people may like to work with others who have similar experiences. Able-bodied men may wish to practise with others to explore ways of dealing with attacks other than the traditional option for men – hitting back harder. So you will need to think in advance about how much it matters to you to learn with a homogeneous group. You may also have a preference for either a man or a woman teacher.

The great value of a class should be the opportunities it provides in a protected, friendly environment, to share experiences, to explore a range of techniques, to practise safely and, finally, to end up being able to do much more than you thought possible at the beginning.

A list of local classes, correct at the time of going to press, is available on request with a 9″ × 4″ stamped addressed envelope from: *Streetwise*, BBC Television, London W12 8QT.

Be safe on the street

The apparently increasing amount of street violence is the main reason that so many people feel nervous about going out alone, although the fear generated by the way these crimes are reported is often out of all proportion to the actual crime rate. There are many simple precautions you can take which will not only transform the way you feel about going out but which will also improve your chances of walking safely once you are on the street. A good many of these attacks are spontaneous – the attackers simply seize an opportunity when they see it. By thinking ahead you will already have gone a long way towards outwitting them.

Often it is hard initially to be sure whether there is danger at all. Some encounters in the street are sexual threats – a man following a woman or calling out after her. Some may involve physical attacks where theft is the aim. Street theft with violence has come to be described as 'mugging', but this is not a legal term. Theft with assault involves rapid, physical attack – a sharp push or trip – so that the attacker can then rob you of your bag or other valuables. Many people who have been attacked in this way say how unexpected it was. The attacker seems to come out of nowhere. Then, after taking what he wants, he seems to run off at such great speed that it is impossible to describe him properly:

> I was just walking along the road minding my own business. It was broad daylight and I wasn't the only person in the street. There were several people about who must have seen everything. Anyway, all of a sudden these two boys ran round the corner. I didn't really catch onto what was happening at all. As they ran past me one knocked into me really hard. I lost my balance and nearly fell over. The other one must have grabbed hold of my bag. I didn't really see them. All I remember is that they both had fair hair. I'd say they were in their teens. I was terribly upset afterwards. I haven't been out all that much since.

It is a frightening experience to be attacked in this way and many people find it hard to regain their confidence afterwards, even if the actual physical harm or the value of the stolen goods was small. Also, because of the speed with which the attack happens and the way in which such attacks are reported in the news-papers, it often seems that you simply do not stand a chance. But here is another story:

> I was walking through the underpass and I saw this boy. I could see that he'd spotted me and that he was dawdling and uncertain. It didn't seem as if he was just aiming to walk straight on past me. As he got to me he grabbed hold of my wrist. I think he must have been after my watch. I turned and faced him and just stood firm. I shouted at him to let me go and I twisted my wrist out of his hold. He looked so surprised. Then he ran off. I was a bit shaken afterwards but I felt really proud of myself.

Obviously it helped in this situation that the woman involved had had some time to assess the situation and to prepare for the possibility of being attacked. Also she was only faced with one attacker. Nevertheless her level of awareness was excellent. She quickly took in a lot of information about the boy and understood the possible significance of his interest in her.

Remember, too, that fear can be your friend. It need not paralyse you so that you are unable to act to protect yourself. Fear prepares your body for action and gives you warning signals which you can usually trust. The ideas we give on pages 11–26 will help you to recognise and use these warning signals in a positive way.

Precautions

Whether dealing with threats of sexual violence or robbery, there are many sensible general precautions you can take.

If you feel anxious about going out alone, is there another way you could travel to feel safer? Is there someone who could accompany you?

Check what you are wearing, as this will affect what you can do in an attack. How much could you move in your clothes and shoes? Could you run? Could you kick? Could you wear more practical shoes and clothes for the journey?

Choose the safest route even if it is not the shortest. Choose well-lit streets at night and keep to the most populated areas, avoiding waste ground and open spaces. Are there people you know living along the route on whom you could call if necessary? Are there busy community centres, familiar pubs, shops, or a police station?

Are you travelling at the safest time? A small change in the time you leave could mean a big difference to how safe you feel.

> When I didn't have my car I tried to travel at Bingo-turning-out-time when there would be a lot of women at bus stops. An hour later, when the pubs empty, the streets feel completely different.

Would you feel safer carrying a whistle, an alarm or a stink bomb to attract attention? If you do carry one you must practise so that you can use it quickly and confidently in an emergency.

Carry any valuables where they are hidden and hard to find. Think about the kind of bag or carrier you are using. A simple clutch bag is easier to steal than a bag worn over the shoulder, but it will not really be worth anyone's while to engage you in a prolonged and difficult struggle to get a bag which is slung diagonally across your chest. (However, be prepared for an attacker who may cut the straps of a bag.) Keep the flap or fastening closed and turned towards your body. If you prefer to carry a bag that you hold in your hand, or under your arm, ask yourself if it is necessary to keep all your most valuable possessions in it. Check before you go out. Do you need your cheque book, your driver's licence, your credit cards or your

Two safe ways to carry a handbag: (left) slung across the chest, flap turned inwards, (right) a bag with a zip held forward and at the point where the zip closes.

unemployment benefit card? These can be tiresome to replace and sometimes it can give you confidence to know that you could just give over the bag without a struggle because there is nothing of any particular value in it. The assured way you hold and handle your bag can be communicated to any would-be attacker too.

Take particular care at banks, cash points and post offices. These are recognised spots for robbery. If you are cashing a cheque, collecting a pension or child benefit, put the money away at the counter and close your bag or replace your wallet safely. Never walk about waving a bulging wad of money, and do not carry a purse or wallet in your hand.

Jewellery has recently become a popular target for attackers. Try to hide any obviously valuable jewellery by keeping your coat fastened and gloves on. You could be hurt if rings or necklaces are snatched from you.

Once you are walking you need to keep yourself both alert and relaxed. You need to notice whatever is going on around you, so that you immediately observe anything strange. For instance, you may pick up small signals about the way someone looks or moves, which in themselves mean nothing but which can warn you of potential danger.

Initially, it may be hard to know what the danger is, if it exists at all. A man approaching you to ask for the time or a light may want just that, or he may be looking for a way to get into conversation. He may want to pass the time of day, or to persuade you to go somewhere with him. He may intend to rob or rape you.

Remember that you have the right to refuse all contact with him. You do not have to give any information or help of any kind. You do not have to tell him anything about yourself. You do not have to be polite or friendly, unless that seems to be the safest tactic. You do not have to put his feelings before your own.

If someone does approach you, do not jump to conclusions but try to keep in your mind all his possible motives and be ready to react to any of them. If you assume that he just wants to chat, you will not be ready if he makes a pass or grabs you. If you assume he intends to hurt you, you may be taken by surprise if he seizes your bag and runs off. If you always assume the worst it can stop you having harmless contact with people, and could leave you tense and ill-prepared if a serious attack actually does happen.

To be alert you need to stay relaxed. Panic freezes your senses and your ability to act. If you notice early warning signs of trouble you are less likely to be caught off guard.

Walk along facing oncoming traffic so that you cannot be taken by surprise by a car creeping alongside you. If a car does draw up near you, keep walking to show that you do not want any contact. If the driver or passenger asks for directions you can:

● ignore them and walk on
● say that you do not know and walk on
● give what help you can, while keeping well out of reach of the car.

If you are being bothered by someone in a car, make a note of the colour, make and registration number. Telling the driver that you have noticed the registration number and will report him may be enough to send him off:

> It was very late one summer night and I was wheeling my bicycle down one side of Clapham Common when a man in a car approached me for directions. I told him I didn't know the road he wanted. He persisted, then made an obscene suggestion over and over again. I didn't know what to do to get rid of him and felt quite frightened. Suddenly, I had an inspiration. I said: 'I can see your registration number and I'm going to report you'. I couldn't see it actually but he zoomed off at top speed!

Walk well away from hedges and entrances where an attacker can hide. Be aware of people in parked cars too. All this may seem a lot to notice at once but you probably do much of it already anyway. Making these simple observations will quickly become second nature and allow you to relax because you are better prepared. One woman used this technique:

> I was out one night really late and had to walk home. I was terrified. So I walked down the middle of the road, pretending to be a panther. I prowled all the way home!

Have your keys where you can reach them quickly. If you have been followed you do not want to fumble on your doorstep. You may decide not to go straight home, but to go somewhere else to get help, or to the police, so that your follower does not know where you live. Another reason for keeping your keys in your hand or pocket is that if your bag is snatched you will still able to get into your house. Also, if your keys are stolen you will have to go to all the trouble and expense of changing your locks.

Walk and move so that you feel strong and relaxed. An attacker will think twice before attacking someone who looks self-assured and ready to stand up for themselves. Obvious physical strength will clearly play a part in deterring an attacker, but many people who are not physically strong still seem impressive in themselves, so it is not essential to be able-bodied and fit.

Notice how you move your body, how you hold your head when you are feeling confident and start to put this into your normal way of moving. In this way you can look confident, even when you are feeling depressed or tired:

> I was walking home through a park at midnight to save time. This was silly I now realise, but it was so late, I was tired and there were no taxis or buses. Two men suddenly appeared from the public lavatory and started circling round and round me. I kept my head up, my back straight and my walk brisk. I appeared to take no notice of them at all. Nothing happened. I'm sure that if I had panicked and run, which was what I felt like doing, they would have attacked me. Pretending confidence must be what prevented it.

We have already said that your voice is one of your first weapons when approached or attacked. It can be hard to find a clear strong voice when you are frightened, so it helps to be ready in case you suddenly need to talk or shout:

> I sing or hum to myself when I'm out on my own. It keeps my voice ready and it makes me feel braver too!

> I practise good one-liners, under my breath. You know, snappy things to say if anyone pesters you. I'm sure people think I'm mad sometimes as I walk along muttering to myself, but it keeps them away!

> I've got a really soft voice and I find it hard to make it sound strong. Once when some bloke was pestering me and being abusive I whispered something abusive back. He automatically said 'What?', and I felt I had gained control because he was asking me for something.

Being followed

If you think you are being approached or followed it is important to act immediately, to check whether it is really happening, to assess the nature of the attack and to prepare for action.

First, check who your follower is and what sort of threat he presents. If you are a woman and realise it is another woman (or a man and a woman) you may feel a sense of relief that you are not the only woman on the street. But if you still feel uneasy, trust your feeling. People are sometimes attacked by women or couples.

When you are sure you are being followed it is time to go onto the alert. Take note of your follower's size and physical state. Does he look drunk? Is he carrying anything which could be used as a weapon? How far away is he? Is he hurrying or loitering? Are there several men or just one? You may feel that glancing over your shoulder shows that you are frightened, but it also gives you much of the information you need to assess the danger.

Check whether you are being followed by crossing over the road, changing pace, or crossing and doubling back on yourself. See if he tries to stay with you.

Take a few seconds to relax. Take long deep breaths in and out; concentrate on relaxing your shoulders, neck and anywhere else that feels particularly tense, so that you are ready to move freely. Relax your voice by humming or practising what you will say if he approaches you.

In your mind run through all the possible courses of action: for instance, changing your route suddenly; running away; asking for help, either from passers-by or by knocking on someone's door; just talking to passers-by so that someone will definitely be there if your follower pesters you; placing yourself near people, maybe at a bus stop; turning and saying something to the person following you; starting to act in an odd way such as talking or laughing to yourself:

> When I was a teenager I was walking down a fairly lonely road in the village one evening when I heard footsteps just behind me. I looked back quickly and there was someone there. He looked 'wrong' somehow. His face seemed 'tight' and he was staring at me, and I didn't recognise him as local. I crossed the road, so did he. I was a long way from home. There was a bungalow just ahead with lights on so I quickly walked up the path and rang the bell, even though I

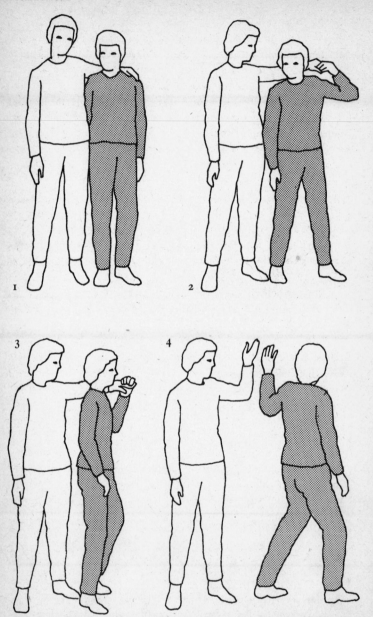

(1, 2) Pick the attacker's hand off your shoulder. (3, 4) Turn round and walk out and away from him.

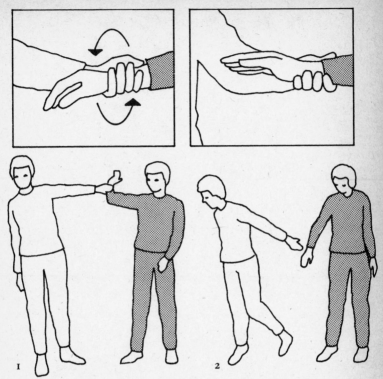

(1) The attacker has grabbed your wrist. His grip is weakest in the gap between the thumbs and index finger. (2) Twist your wrist towards this gap and pull out of the hold.

didn't know who lived there. The awful thing was they were out – must have left the lights on to give the impression that the house was occupied. However, it was enough to get rid of the man. I stayed there, shaking like a leaf for ages until I heard nothing. As I emerged from the house I saw him walking back towards the village so he had definitely been up to no good.

Everybody should take responsibility for not frightening other people. This can happen without you realising it – for example, if you are walking too closely behind someone, or by making what may seem to you friendly conversation. This is especially true if you are a man walking behind or talking to a woman you do not know. Cross the road to make it clear you are not following, or walk at a different pace.

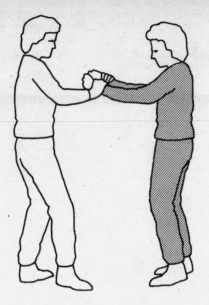

I

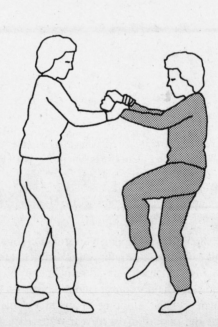

2

(1) An attacker has grabbed your wrists. (2) Use his hold to balance yourself.

3
(3) Now kick to his shins – this kick is more appropriate when you are wearing shoes which protect your toes.

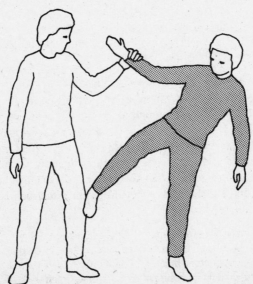

Alternatively, use the attacker's hold to give you balance. A sideways kick to the attacker's knee uses the side of your foot to make the strike.

Theft with assault ('Mugging')

There are no hard and fast rules for coping with a street theft. Some people have preferred to give up their possessions rather than risk being hurt:

> I was coming out of my local bus station when someone attacked me and his accomplice tried to take my bag. At first, I clung to it, but the first man started hurting me and hissing threats about what would happen. I valued not getting hurt above my bag, so I let it go.

Sometimes it is even possible to bargain with a thief, as this man did:

> I was visiting my cousins one very dark, cold winter night. I went to my car and had just opened the car door when two men appeared. One of them threw me over the car bonnet and said 'You smashed my brother's car – look, it's damaged.' It was true that the car behind was damaged, but obviously this was nothing to do with me. A third man appeared and grabbed me round the throat. 'You've got to give us £50', he said. I felt very cool, so I said 'O.K. boys, let's negotiate about this.' One of them grabbed my wallet. It had two £20 notes in it. I said 'Now look, boys, it's a cold night – you wouldn't want to leave me penniless, would you?' They took one of the £20 notes and left the other. They went off up the street cackling and saying 'What a sucker!' But actually the last laugh was on them. My cousin had just given me £570 in cash to bank the next morning, and this was in my trouser pocket the whole time!

Another possible tactic when confronted by someone who demands your bag is to fling your bag at him so that the contents scatter. He will have to crouch to retrieve them, giving you time to run. This is especially useful when the attacker is armed.

However, it is also true that many people have held on to their possessions and driven off their attackers not only because of the sheer anger and outrage they feel at being personally attacked in this way, but *because* their money or jewellery felt too precious to let go:

> I was stopped by a young man as I was coming out of the station one night. He demanded all my money and my rings. I wouldn't have cared much about the money as I didn't have much with me. But I was damned if he was going to have my rings which were all left to me by my mother. I shouted 'How dare you' at him, and 'Go away, I'll call the Police' and he just melted away.

(1) An attacker has pushed you against a wall. (2) You can use the wall as a support. (3) Now you push against his chest. You could combine this with a strike to a vulnerable part of the body.

47

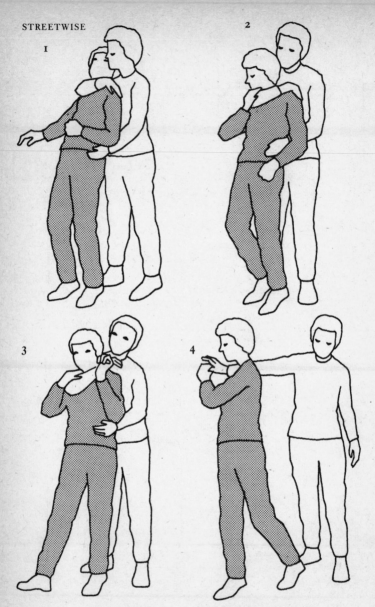

(1) The attacker has grabbed you from behind with his arm round your neck. (2) Move the attacker's arm so that you can tuck your chin into the crook of his arm. This protects your windpipe. (3) Pick up the attacker's little finger and bend it back. If necessary keep pushing down on his elbow joint with your other hand. (4) Pull the little finger and open the attacker's hold, then move away.

Pickpockets

Pickpocketing does not usually involve a frightening assault. The essence of pickpocketing is that your handbag, purse or wallet is stolen with such light fingers that you do not feel it go. However, losing all your money and credit cards is still an extremely upsetting experience. Cash is not insurable, and your credit cards will need to be cancelled and your cheques stopped. Some credit cards (for instance, those from a department store) may include your address so you may feel you also have to change your locks. Again, as with other self-defence situations, prevention is more than half the battle.

Well-practised intuition can sometimes tell you when a pickpocket is searching for a victim. He or she will be the person who is not looking at the goods in a market, but is looking at the shoppers. The pickpocket may be carrying a shopping bag but no shopping; he may be wearing a baggy raincoat with deep pockets.

Much pickpocketing is casual and unplanned but many pickpockets also work 'professionally' in teams of between two and twenty. Their success depends on their power to distract your attention long enough to take your property.

One method of operation is to have someone approach you from the front. They may bump into you, push you, cough at you or perhaps start an argument. While this is going on, the accomplice will open your bag, and take your purse or wallet, then pass it to a third person who will disappear quickly into a crowd.

If you are waiting for a bus or tube in the rush hour a large team of pickpockets may use another approach. A member of the team will block the entrance of the bus, perhaps by arguing with the conductor. The passengers will push to get off and the queue will surge forward to get on. Everyone will be pushed closely together and the pickpockets will take valuables unnoticed.

A pickpocket is often well-trained to open a bag and take a purse in a matter of seconds. If there is a crowd the pickpocket will seek out people who look the easiest 'marks'. Your best defence is to make sure you are not the one who stands out. Looking alert and being aware of the danger is a good principle.

If you are carrying a lot of money think about putting it in several different places. It is always better to have just enough money handy for your immediate needs and no more. Be careful if you are writing a cheque in a busy shop. Keep hold of your bag and keep it closed, otherwise you may find your purse stolen while you are concentrating on the cheque. Never leave a purse lying on top of an open shopping basket.

It is better to avoid leaving wallets in back pockets where a professional pickpocket can take them. Men may protest that they would immediately notice a hand in a back pocket. This may be true, but by the time they had noticed, the pickpocket and the wallet would be far away. If a wallet is in an inside coat pocket, then fasten the jacket. Try not to put anything of value in rain-coat pockets. If you carry a shoulder bag with a zip, pull the zip to the front rather than the back of the bag and grasp it as you walk along. Bags with flaps should be turned towards the body. In any case try to remember to hold the bag tightly against your body. Pickpockets often go to discos and dances:

> I was at a disco where it was the custom for all the girls to put their bags in a pile. The theory was we'd keep an eye on them that way. Unfortunately, one night several people lost bags. The thief must have walked past, casually hooked out a bag and walked on. The cluster of bags looked safe, but it wasn't. I never take a good bag to a disco now, and I always try to keep it with me at all times.

It is also possible to have a bag stolen from the floor at a cinema. The best place for a bag is on your lap, otherwise think whether you need to take one with you at all. Similarly bags can also be stolen from under the adjacent cubicle wall in a lavatory. Use the hook provided – do not leave your bag on the floor.

In a cafe or restaurant the bag is often hung by its strap on the back of the seat. In this situation a pickpocket may come to your table and will make you feel uncomfortable. He may reach for salt and pepper, knock things over or argue with you. When you are feeling relieved that he has gone, you will turn round and find that your bag has gone with him.

The worst part of a wallet or purse theft is often the object of sentimental value that has been taken with the money. The cash you can eventually replace but not mementoes and photographs. There is a slim chance of retrieving them. Many pickpockets go straight to the nearest public lavatory, take your credit cards, cheque books and cash, then put your purse or wallet in either the lavatory cistern or the waste bin. If your property has been taken it is always worth looking in nearby bins and lavatories.

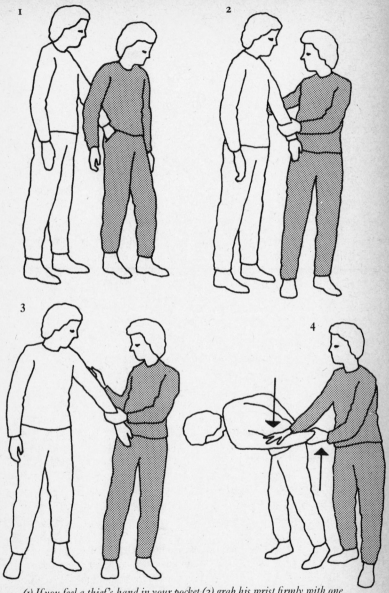

(1) If you feel a thief's hand in your pocket (2) grab his wrist firmly with one hand; (3) push your other hand hard into the back of his elbow; (4) pull his wrist up, pushing his elbow down and force him away from you; retrieve your belongings.

Travelling safely

Public transport

Attacks which happen on public transport are similar to attacks on the street: pickpocketing, arguments which turn into fights, sexist or racist comments which may turn into a more serious assault, women being 'touched up' by men standing or sitting too close to them, indecent exposure, and so on. The difference is that you are in a confined space. This makes it harder to refuse to enter into a conversation or argument than if you could walk away quickly. Remember, though, it often *is* possible to move away from someone who is bothering you.

> A man came and sat next to me, taking up three quarters of the seat and squashing me up against the window, while the rest of the bus was half empty. I started to shrink away into the smallest space possible. Then suddenly I felt really angry. I gathered up my bags, stood up and asked him to move. He wanted me to squeeze past him and that made me even more certain that he was touching me up. I made him move and went to sit somewhere else. The woman in front turned round and commiserated with me about how pushy some men are, which was wonderful because I had felt so embarrassed about making such a fuss.

Another difference from street attacks is that there are often other people around. This can be either a source of support or of embarrassment.

> I was standing on the tube, in the rush hour. I hate that anyway, you get so squashed and jostled. Suddenly I felt a hand between my legs. I turned round and looked at the men standing behind me. They all looked distant and shut off, you know that glazed look people get in crowds. They all looked normal, respectable men going home after a hard day at the office. It was me who was embarrassed and confused. I couldn't tell who had done it and I felt too ashamed and embar-

rassed to say anything. But what right have they got to do that to me? What goes on in their minds?

One woman dealt magnificently with a 'groper' by feeling for the intrusive hand, seizing it, lifting it up and crying loudly: 'Whose hand is this?' Some people don't hesitate to shout and confront their attacker:

> I was going down the escalator and I heard a woman shouting. A small crowd had gathered round. She was shouting at a man standing near her: 'How dare you touch me! You're pathetic! You're disgusting! I'm sick of men thinking they can treat us like this! You try and shame me into silence but you won't . . .' She continued shouting while the crowd walled him in, until someone from London Transport came and hauled him off. I hope I'll have the courage to do the same if it happens to me.

Precautions
First, you should practise the same detailed observation and general tactics that we have recommended for the street. Keep alert and look confident. Make sure that you know where the exits are: it may give you confidence to sit near them. Try to choose a compartment with plenty of other people in it. If you begin to feel isolated in a train, don't hesitate to move to a more populated carriage.

Sometimes it helps to start up conversations with people who look friendly. Nothing elaborate is necessary – a simple remark about the weather will do. If other people do not wish to talk, then, of course, you must respect their wish to be silent. This is especially important if you are a man starting up a conversation with a woman. Remember that she does not know your intentions in chatting to her. Many women tell of being trapped in friendly conversations with men they did not know:

> He was just chatting away. I chatted back a bit, because I didn't know how to stop the conversation without be rude. I tried a couple of times, by turning away or not really responding to what he said, but he didn't seem to notice. He didn't *do* anything, just said goodbye when he got off the bus. But it was night-time, there weren't many people around, and I had to spend the whole journey on my guard, just in case it developed into the kind of situation you read about in the papers. I'm sure he didn't give it a second thought!

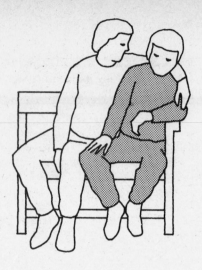

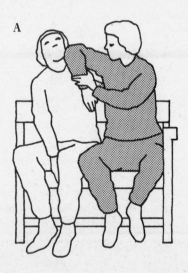

A

A man puts an unwanted arm round your shoulder. You can (A) bring your elbow up sharply under his chin. Gripping your wrist with the other hand will give the strike more force.

B

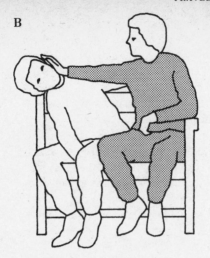

C

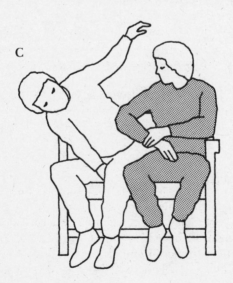

Or you can (B) place the palm of your hand against his face and push until your arm is straight. This action throws him off balance. Or (C) elbow him sharply in the ribs. Try to move away quickly afterwards.

So if you are a man, take care not to frighten people in an attempt to be friendly. In an empty bus or train, don't sit next to, or directly opposite a woman on her own. Don't expect her to want to talk or be friendly.

If you feel threatened by anyone, trust your intuition and act as soon as you feel uneasy. Too often people wait, becoming more and more uneasy, until they are sure that danger is there. Usually, this means waiting until it is too late to prevent an attack. Remember that if you take preventative action early enough the attack may not happen. You may feel that you made a fool of yourself in the process, but remember that you acted on the feeling that you were in danger. You made the sensible choice that you would risk looking foolish rather than risk being hurt.

Early warning signals to look out for are:
- somebody sitting or standing uncomfortably close to you
- someone persisting in an unwelcome conversation
- seeing a row or fight developing between other people
- seeing or hearing someone being abusive to you, other passengers, the conductor or ticket collector
- groups of people being noisy or messing about.

Find the guard or ticket collector, or enlist the help of other passengers if you have time. On trains be prepared to use the emergency cord if you or others are in danger.

Indecent exposure

Indecent exposure or 'flashing' is when a man shows his penis to a woman or child. It often happens in parks, quiet streets or on public transport. Sometimes a man rubs his penis and becomes sexually aroused while looking at a woman or women near him, or at obscene magazines in a public place.

Indecent exposers rely on your being shocked, embarrassed and confused. They rely on you to keep quiet. Women often feel angry, frightened or ashamed. Sometimes they even feel, illogically, that they have somehow provoked the man.

When a man is exposing himself you may wish just to turn your back or move away. If there are other women around, see whether any of them have noticed or are looking upset. They may help you to stop him. They may need help themselves. Most importantly, try not to give him the reaction he wants. Almost any other reaction will throw him off balance and give you control of the situation:

> I couldn't stop laughing. He looked so stupid sitting there with his little willie, looking all intent. Me and my friend just shrieked with laughter and he put it away.

> I just told him to put it away, it wasn't worth showing off.

> I stared him out, I completely ignored his hands. Just stared into his face until he got up and moved.

> I pretended not to notice until the train stopped. Then I stood on the platform and told everyone not to get in that carriage because there was a man in there exposing himself. Then I told the guard.

> My son noticed and asked in a loud voice what that man was doing. I answered him in an equally loud voice, explaining to the whole carriage that he was a strange man who wanted to show everyone his penis, and that we would have to call the guard if he didn't stop. Everyone stared, first at me and then at him. I was glad I had previously explained to Tim about 'flashers'. As it was, I felt very embarrassed and not sure if I couldn't have reacted better. But I was glad I had done something. And glad that Tim had seen me not just put up with it.

If you are alone in a bus or train carriage with a man who is exposing himself or sexually arousing himself you have to decide more carefully how to deal with it. You could sit away from him until you can leave at the next stop. Most importantly, you will have to weigh up whether there is more serious danger. Your judgement will be based on what you have noticed or felt intuitively about him. It will also depend on how far you have to go before the next stop. Most indecent exposers are not dangerous. They are more likely to be filled with guilt about what they are doing. In any situation where you feel that this is *not* the case, trust the feeling and act accordingly: prepare to defend yourself against more serious attack.

Cars

In this section we look at what women can do when trapped in a car with someone who is threatening violence, or who tries to make offensive conversation. Cars are the most common places where these situations arise, but they may also occur in offices or other places where running away or shouting for help is not always possible as a first line of defence. You may find yourself in this situation with a stranger. It is more common, and often more embarrassing, when it happens with someone you know.

Conversations may start innocently, but can quickly become unpleasant and uncomfortable. For example, an apparently innocent question about whether or not you are married or have a boyfriend can easily lead into suggestions about your sexual availability. It can be deliberately used to place you in a false position where you find yourself having to prove that you were not teasing or 'leading him on'.

The same thing goes for 'innocent' conversations about money or about the clothes you are wearing. These conversations in themselves can be offensive and undermining and also may contain a threat of further danger.

Sometimes the threat can be subtle. The man relies on your fear of 'over-reacting' or causing an embarrassing scene. He can respond if you do by making you look a fool: 'You must be a bit desperate if you think I'd fancy you', or 'Aren't you touchy? It was only a joke'. You may feel powerless and threatened in a situation which a man feels is just a game.

However, it is perfectly possible to defend yourself, sometimes in somewhat unconventional ways:

> I was once in a train in Germany. I can't really speak German but a German man in the carriage began to chat to me. I smiled and nodded a lot because I couldn't talk. Within a few minutes he stopped being pleasant and became really threatening. I couldn't fight him off so I pretended to retch violently. He looked disgusted and moved off. Another time, when a bloke in a car was being offensive, I picked my nose and wiped snot on his windscreen. Truly a good way to lose 'friends'!

These situations can be especially difficult where the man has some kind of 'authority' over the woman:

My driving instructor kept putting his hand on my thigh. It was excruciatingly embarrassing – I could feel myself getting red – after all it could have been just friendly. Also I felt I was in his power because I was only a learner and not doing very well at that! I thought about it all week. When he did it again, I stopped the car and said: 'Look, I'm sure you don't mean any harm, but it's so distracting having your hand there – will you remove it please?' He looked stunned, then annoyed, and said: 'You shouldn't wear those tight trousers'. What a nerve – they weren't tight anyway. I complained to the school and they gave me a different instructor.

Another woman was hitching a lift:

I didn't like the driver much but I thought he was probably all right. I could hardly believe it when he suddenly said: 'I'll put you off where you want if you let me look down your blouse'. Fortunately I got him to stop and I just jumped out and slammed the door.

It is easy to think: 'Oh no, I'm sure he's joking', to keep on giving him the benefit of the doubt because you cannot believe that anyone could be so unpleasant. Unfortunately, you need to realise that there are some men who enjoy these situations. They know they frighten women and they are excited by exerting their power.

When you accept a lift with someone or you invite them into your car, try to start off by being clear about the 'deal' you are making. For example, it is a good idea with someone you do not know well to be absolutely clear about your destination and when you expect to get there. You could say that you are expected at a specific time. This can put your relationship with your driver or passenger on a business-like level right at the beginning.

Try to keep control over the conversation if you feel at all worried. Remember you do not have to put up with offensive conversation once it starts. There will almost certainly be moments when you can turn it and regain control.

Remember that no one has the right to intimidate you – you do not owe favours to someone who has bought you a meal or offered you a lift. You do not have to go on being pleasant to someone who is deliberately setting out to frighten you.

Trust your intuition. If you start to feel threatened or embarrassed then it probably means that something threatening or embarrassing is happening. If you 'over-react' or make a fool of yourself the worst you have done is just that. You do not have to explain yourself.

Feel free to talk or behave in any way that will make you feel safer. You have the right to change the conversation, you have the right not to hear what has been said, you can tell lies if you need to, or you can behave in a strange or unpleasant way.

> 'Your boyfriend's a lucky man.'
> *'Lovely weather we're having for the time of year, isn't it?'*

or

> 'Your boyfriend's a lucky man.'
> *'I want you to stop the car right now. I want to get out.'*

There is also the possibility of using naïvety as a positive form of self-defence, for instance pretending not to notice what you are being drawn into, making him feel inadequate by refusing to understand his hints, or turning down his offers as if you were turning down a cup of tea.

Women have been brought up to think that other people's feelings are more important than their own. Learn to recognise when someone is undermining your confidence or being rude. You do not have to feel sorry for someone who is upsetting you.

You can also take action yourself if the situation looks dangerous. For instance, you might jump out at red traffic lights, or wind down the window to shout for help. It is dangerous to seize the handbrake, but FAILING ALL ELSE in some situations you might simply open the passenger door (remaining strapped in yourself, of course). It is extremely difficult to drive when a passenger door is flapping loose. Obviously you would not want to do this in a busy street where the door might injure passers-by.

You could also try appealing to a potential attacker on human terms:

> I was in Switzerland in winter and arrived at my friend's apartment block unexpectedly a day early. It was 1.00 a.m. and unfortunately she was away.
>
> I decided to look for an hotel, but it was a residential district. I noticed three middle-aged men and a car down the street – they'd obviously just finished a good night out. One man was getting in and the others were saying goodnight. I asked them to help me. They

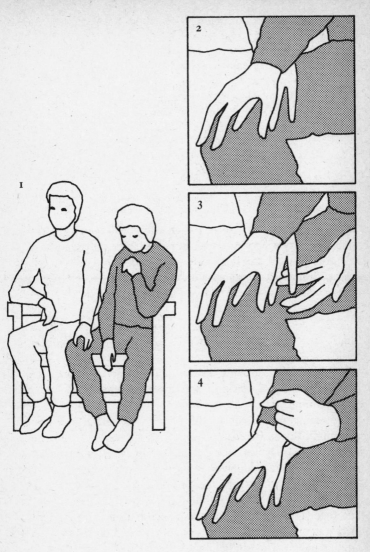

(1) A man has put an unwanted hand on your knee. (2) Place either hand over his hand, leaving his little finger free. (3) Grasp his little finger firmly with your other hand. You can look into his face to distract him from your action. (4) Holding his hand down, pull his little finger up sharply to cause pain. Remove his hand. Practise this very carefully because you can easily damage the finger.

agreed to drive me to an hotel. To my surprise the other two men got in too. In a very short time I realised they were talking and making lewd jokes about me and the car was speeding from the hotel district. In my bad German I suddenly asked the driver if he was married. 'Yes.' Had he got a daughter? 'Yes.' How old was she? 'Seventeen.' So I said, 'If your daughter was alone in a foreign country like this, what would you do?' He suddenly looked shame-faced, and in no time at all we were outside an hotel. He helped me out with my suitcase and shook my hand.

Advice to drivers

When you are driving yourself there are several precautions you can take to ensure a safer journey.

Keep all the doors locked when you are driving – attackers sometimes try to force a way in by wrenching open a door. Keep the doors locked and the windows up even if you are stationary and waiting for someone. For ventilation you can open the driver's-side window a crack at the top or use quarter-lights if you have them.

Lock your car and close the windows even if you are only leaving it for a few moments, and check that no-one is concealed inside on your return. Always have your keys ready to use immediately. If you can, choose well-lit, busy car parks. On-street parking in a well-populated road is probably safer than a multi-storey car park, especially at night.

It is sometimes possible to be followed by another motorist. If you think this is happening you could try some of the tactics described earlier for being followed on foot. For instance, changing routes suddenly then looking to see if the other car is still behind. It is probably better not to try zooming away and playing dodgems – you could endanger yourself and others on the road. Drive steadily to a busy area and make straight for a police station, a friend's house, or somewhere you can be sure of finding people who can help.

If you are a woman, be generous with your car in offering lifts to other women who may be stranded or have difficult journeys after meetings or parties. In general, as with other kinds of self-defence, you must trust your instinct in offering lifts to men. It is probably sensible for women not to give lifts to male hitch-hikers or to motorists who appear to have broken down.

Be safe at home

Your home is only your castle if you have taken some trouble to make it safe against intruders, who may be peeping toms, burglars or even rapists. Some intruders are more dangerous than others, but any unwanted entry into your home can be upsetting and disturbing. Whatever their intentions, intruders are better kept out.

There are some simple steps you can take to accomplish this. Most of the physical precautions are not expensive and do not require any great DIY skill to install. Remember, though, that there is no such thing as an impregnable home. Your precautions have two purposes. First, they deter the casual intruder looking for easy targets. Secondly, if he is determined to get in, they buy you time – with luck – to discover him and summon help.

The precautions we list in this section are only suggestions. You will need to think how much you can afford, and also how far you want or need to make your house a fortress.

Precautions
Locks
Strong locks are expensive and usually need to be installed by a locksmith, but they are a good investment. Front and back doors need mortice deadlocks conforming to British Standard 3621. A five-lever lock is the strongest, if you can afford it. Try to get into the habit of double-locking your door on leaving the house.

Do not leave a back door key in the lock. A burglar could break a window then extract the key. Do not leave your key on a string inside the letter box, under a mat or flower pot, or on a ledge. These are the first places an intruder will search.

Window locks are comparatively cheap. There is one to suit every type of frame, including french doors. Be aware that you

Window lock with a key

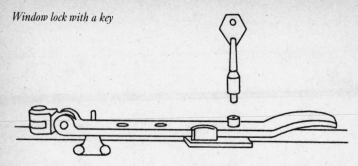

may be creating a fire trap by preventing your windows from opening easily. This can also be a problem with metal grilles and double-glazing, both of which are good precautions against burglary. Everyone in the house should know where the window keys are kept and how to use them.

Small but strong metal screws are available which can be fixed to windows so that they only open about six inches for air. To open them further they need a key. These screws are cheap and simple to install. They are a useful defence against intrusion in bedrooms at night.

It is particularly important to protect basement windows as they so often provide both accessibility and the opportunity to force an entry unseen.

Doors

Good locks will not necessarily protect you if the door and its frame are weak. Hinges should be strong and well-concealed.

You can buy a door-viewer so that you can inspect every caller before even opening the door. You should also have a light over your door, so that you can still see callers in the dark.

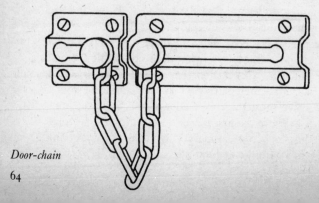

Door-chain

A strong door-chain is a good idea as it can be used to answer the door to someone you do not recognise. (Door-chains are not suitable where the door opening is immediately adjacent to a wall, as there is no space for you to see the caller.)

Keep internal doors closed but not locked. If you do have a burglar he could do a great deal of damage at his leisure breaking down doors. However, closed doors will probably create doubt and uncertainty in his mind about what lies behind them.

Lights

Most burglaries happen during the day, but there are intruders who like to work in the dark. You can now buy vandal-proof 'bulkhead' lights to fix over porches and backdoors or windows which can remain on all night. When you go out at night a time-switch can turn your lights on for you. This makes the house appear occupied. Turning lights on in a bedroom and a down-stairs room is a more convincing sign of occupation than leaving on the hall lights.

Alarm systems

Complete alarm systems are expensive to install and you would need professional advice on the choice and maintenance of the right system for your home. There are so many false alarms that many passers-by automatically ignore every alarm bell, including some which are genuine. Some people feel that buying the bell box alone is sufficient to deter a potential intruder. Others like the confidence which a complex system gives them. If you are in doubt about whether an alarm system is a good idea for your home, you could contact the Crime Prevention Officer at your local police station for free advice.

Visibility

Do not leave windows or doors uncurtained if people can easily look through from the road or garden to see if you are there or not. A cheap net curtain or frosted glass will obscure their view and make them less certain of your movements. Keep your cur-tains drawn properly on dark evenings.

Identification

Make a descriptive list of your valuables and note any serial numbers. Thieves sometimes remove serial numbers on stolen property, so you might also discreetly scratch your initials inside any electrical equipment. You can also buy a marking pen which only shows up under special light. This is relatively expensive, but could be worthwhile if, for instance, you have a lot of delicate and valuable china or furniture.

Roofs

Some houses, particularly terraced ones, are vulnerable to entry via the roof: from parapets, through skylights, or by removing broken slates and tiles to gain entry to a loft. Loft doors, skylights and parapet windows should be locked or bolted as appropriate.

In general do not leave ladders, garden tools or screwdrivers lying around outside where they could help an intruder gain access. Cancel your milk and newspapers if you are going away and be discreet about your holiday plans. A friend who can visit your house or flat while you are away to draw curtains and put lights on may satisfactorily confuse someone watching with burglary in mind.

Con men

'If in doubt, keep them out.'

Most callers are perfectly genuine, but there are a few unscrupulous people, men, women or even children, who will not hesitate to use tricks to enter your home.

Always use your door-viewer or door-chain to identify a caller.

Always ask to inspect the identity card of someone who claims to represent the gas, electricity or water boards, British Telecom, the local council, or a market research organisation. If they do not have identity cards or if you feel uneasy, tell them you will telephone their headquarters while they wait outside. All *bona fide* callers should be prepared to do this.

A man knocked at my door and said he was from the Council and had to look at my house because the area was being re-rated. I was immediately suspicious, as I felt sure the Council would have written to me first. So I said 'Can I see your identification please?' He said

'Oh yes, of course' and searched his pockets. 'Oh dear,' he said, 'I seem to have left it at the office – but I'm perfectly genuine, you know'. I replied, 'I'm sorry, I can't let you in without it'. He tried to argue that they'd be very annoyed but I stood firm and closed the door. He didn't return and a week later the local paper had a story about a con man with just his story who had been stealing cash once he was in people's houses.

Some thieves purport to be 'dealers'. They may offer to buy some furniture at a high price in order to offer you a low price for something genuinely valuable. Alternatively, they may be making a 'recce' for a later burglary. When you want to sell an object, it is better to take it to a reputable dealer for valuation. Another common ploy is the bogus workman who tells you that your roof needs instant repair because the Council say it is dangerous, or that he has come to check the water pressure because the main is to be rebuilt . . .

It is important to remember that most of the thieves who choose this method are plausible. They do not look like obvious burglars or attackers. However, quite often there is some small give-away. The 'body-language' may not be totally convincing, the patter may be too slick, he may just seem over-pressing. If you have any doubts at all, trust your instincts and close the door. Telephone your local police station and report the incident. It is better to do this and risk the embarassment of being wrong than to be one more victim of the con man.

Intruders

It might sometimes be a good idea to pretend you are not alone in the house if a stranger calls. Shout back along the hall, 'No, it's OK, I'll get it'. You do not always have to answer the door. But remember that a burglar or attacker who finds a door-bell unanswered may slip round the back to break in there. Some people prefer to shout through the door to find out who it is.

We have already advised making a practice of having the key ready when you return home to avoid fumbling on the doorstep. Once the door is open it is better to go in and close it straight behind you. If you have to empty your waste bin in a passageway, or pop out to see neighbours, shut the door behind you, even if someone else is in the house. It only takes a few seconds for an intruder to slip in and steal your valuables or attack you when you return.

You may come home to find that your key will not open the door. It is extremely likely, in this case, that you have a burglar. He has put down the catch on your lock to protect himself, and has escaped through another door or window. Alternatively, you may find your door gaping open. Do not attempt to enter your house. Use a neighbour's telephone or a call box to ring the police.

It is often best to allow a burglar to leave without a physical confrontation. How you do this will, as in every other kind of self-defence, depend on you and your assessment of what is happening.

One 74-year-old woman found that her anger sustained her in an extremely alarming situation:

> I woke up one night to find a youngish man standing over my bed telling me my friend needed me. I thought at first in my sleepy state that my friend [the same age as herself] had been taken ill. I went down the corridor to find my friend lying in bed speechless with fright. He had already taken £10 from her and threatened to kill her. He ordered me to get into bed with her and he had the key of the room in his hand. He was obviously intending to lock us both in while he ransacked the house. Suddenly, I felt a huge rage. I said very tartly: 'What do you want?' He didn't answer. So I said: 'Out of my house, out, out, out!' I chased him down the stairs and he ran off – but not before giving back my friend's £10. I don't know how I got the courage to do it, but looking at him, I suddenly felt that perhaps he was a bit 'simple' so I took the risk.

Another woman was alone in the day-time when she heard an intruder. She did not have a telephone, but she turned her television, radio and stereo on full blast and opened her windows. It took five minutes for the neighbours to come over to complain. The would-be thief ran off and the only damage was a broken rear window.

Some people have successfully pretended that they were not alone. In a recent armed raid on a post-office, the three thieves ran off when the postmaster told them that there were two more people with dogs in the building, even though this was untrue.

It may also be important to bide your time. Don't feel that you necessarily have to do something straight away. One 13-year-old boy was alone in a house while it was being burgled. The thieves

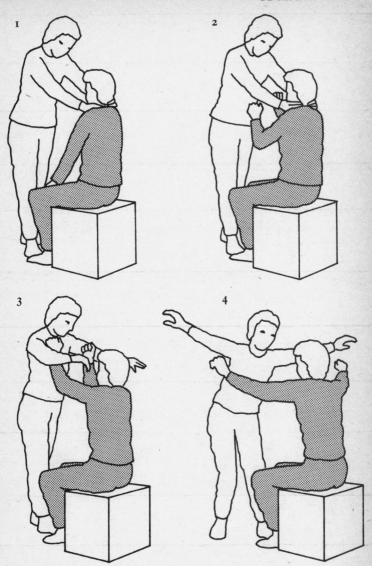

(1) The attacker puts his hands around your throat when you are seated. Lean back slightly to relieve the pressure of his hands on your windpipe. (2) Clench your fists and bring your arms up between your attacker's arms. (3) Push your forearms strongly against the inside of his arms. (4) Force his arms apart as powerfully as you can.

1

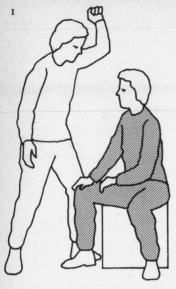

2

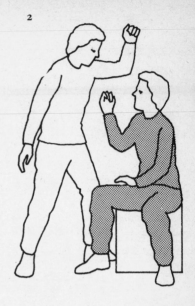

3

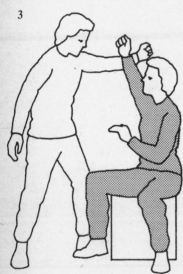

(1) The attacker has his arm raised to strike you. (2) Bring up the arm nearest the attacker, clenching the fist. (3) As his blow comes down, push his arm away strongly with your forearm. You can use this block even if the attacker attempts to strike you with a stick or club. Remember to block against his arm, not the weapon.

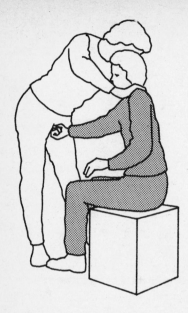

You are seated and the attacker is leaning over you. You are in an ideal position to bring your fist up to hit his testicles hard.

locked him in one room and told him to keep quiet. He waited until he heard them in the top part of the house then flung the window open and yelled for help at the top of his voice. The burglars were caught red-handed.

Remember that the intruder may be as frightened as you are, though you cannot count on it. If you can, offer him some 'peaceful' way out.

I was alone one Sunday afternoon in our big house. I don't know why but I suddenly felt there was something wrong – the hairs on the back of my neck stood up – that sort of thing. I was at the top of the house so I very gingerly came down to the sitting room. I opened the door and came face to face with a complete stranger. I felt my voice go stiff and high and it felt far away but I said: 'Oh, good afternoon, you must be from the electricity board. Is everything all right?' He nodded dumbly. So I said, 'Well, if the meters are fine, perhaps you'd like to leave by the front door'. He nodded again. I showed him out, slammed the door and immediately rang the police. It turned out he had forced the back door, and he was already wanted for theft with violence. I've still no idea what made me think of saying what I did, but I'm sure it saved me from harm.

In the most famous recent example of a bedroom intruder, the

Queen awoke to find a man standing at her bedside. She must have been shocked and alarmed but she did not panic. Perhaps her lifetime's training for her 'job' helped her. She quickly trusted her instinct that Michael Fagan wished her no physical harm. She talked to him calmly about his family, eventually summoning help by offering him a cigarette and calling for her maid to bring one. She emerged from the ordeal physically unharmed.

Obscene telephone calls

Obscene telephone calls are an unwelcome and disturbing intrusion into your home especially when the caller is persistent. It is important to know that most obscene telephone calls are simply an aid to masturbation. No actual physical harm is intended to the recipient. He hopes to surprise or shock you into going on listening to him.

A persistent caller can be dealt with in several ways. You could put the telephone down immediately the obscenity starts. The same applies to 'silent' callers and 'heavy breathers'. If they do not identify themselves, hang up straight away. You could also say a few sharp words before ringing off.

Some people recommend having a whistle or alarm handy and blasting this into your telephone. However, this could damage the caller's hearing, so you have to be very sure first that you can face doing this, and secondly that you have identified the caller correctly.

In seriously intrusive cases ring the exchange and ask for your calls to be intercepted. It is also possible to change your number and become ex-directory, but this is a nuisance for you and your friends. Mostly, however, simply hanging up every time is enough to discourage obscene callers. It denies them the thrill they are seeking.

Women should avoid putting their first names in the telephone directory. Use initials only with no Miss or Mrs to identify you as a woman.

Rape and sexual assault

The legal definition of rape is 'The unlawful carnal knowledge of a female by force or fraud against her will'. Carnal knowledge means penetration of the labia (outer lips of the vagina) by the penis to any degree – full penetration and ejaculation need not take place in order to prove rape.

This is a purely technical and biological definition. The reality of rape is that it is a crime often committed with other kinds of horrifying violence, but in any case rape in itself is a violent act. Rape can also occur within a marriage, though this is not an offence recognised by the law.

Rape is a crime with devastating consequences for the woman who suffers it. She may find herself accused of lying by both her family and her attacker; almost invariably there are no witnesses to support her version of what happened. If her attacker is found and taken to court, rape is the only crime where the character of the *defendant* is, in effect, also on trial. Judges have frequently been known to give a rapist an insultingly light sentence because of their view of the woman's character. The courts put her in an almost impossible double bind. If she has taken police advice, which is not to struggle, she is accused of having given her consent, because there is no evidence that she objected.

After the rape, whether or not there is a court case, the victim is inevitably deeply shaken and upset. Her self-confidence often shattered, she may feel guilty and tainted. She may find it difficult to live a normal life again – to go shopping, to answer the telephone, to visit friends, or to have a loving sexual relationship for some time to come.

Current attitudes towards rape are a legacy from the time when a man actually owned his wife and family. The rape laws were originally intended to protect *a man* from the violation and, therefore, the loss of value of his 'property' by other men. Even now this attitude survives. A single woman who does not clearly 'belong' to another man is much more vulnerable in court than a 'respectable' married woman.

Sometimes women are encouraged to think that they share the blame for the rape. But the truth is that no woman is guilty of being raped. It is every woman's right to refuse sex.

There are some small signs that the situation is slowly improving. The 'rape' episode in the BBC television series *Police* aroused such public outcry that many police forces have now improved the way they deal with rape survivors. Also, there seems to be a trend towards much heavier sentences for rape. Women's groups have put rape on the agenda for public discussion, and organisations like Rape Crisis have set up centres to offer real support to women who have been raped.

Popular myths

There is much confused and mostly erroneous thinking about rape. Perhaps this is because, until recently, rape was a totally taboo subject, rarely reported in newspapers, seldom discussed at home. Here are some of the myths we hear most often:

'Rape is a crime committed by sexually frustrated, or oversexed men.'

It is not true that men have uncontrollable sexual urges. Men are not insatiable beasts. They are members of the community in which we all live, and they have a responsibility to behave towards women with respect and sensitivity.

In studies carried out on convicted rapists, it was found that their sexual drives were in a 'normal' range compared with other men from a cross-section of the community. The difference was in their general level of violence and aggression. They were not 'insane', 'perverted' or 'monsters' . . . just 'normal' men.

In one study of rape in war, it was found that even though soldiers in battle had access to brothels in their own camps, they still tortured, raped and murdered 'enemy' women in large numbers – they were despoiling the enemy's 'property'.

Rape is an act of aggression. The rapist asserts his own power and domination through his sexuality. He intends to humiliate and degrade his victim.

'If you go out on your own late at night you are asking for it.'

Many people claim that any woman out after dark, knowing that she runs the risk of being raped, is deliberately setting herself up as a potential victim. This is not true. Women have the right to walk where they want to, when they want to and should not have to live their lives under curfew. Many women now do not go out at night for fear of being raped. They are prisoners in their own homes, afraid to be out on the streets.

'Rape is committed by strangers who emerge from out of an unlit alley.'

The truth is that women are much more likely to be raped by a man they know. 47% of reported rapes are committed by an acquaintance or a relative. 30% of rapes are committed in the woman's home, and 17% in the rapist's home. And these are only the figures for *reported* rapes. The statistics also reflect the fact that women are less likely to report a rape by a man they know.

'Rape is caused by women who dress provocatively.'

This is not true. Rape survivors include women of all ages and backgrounds. Babies two months old have been raped and so have nuns and women in their nineties. It does not make any difference if women are wearing pretty clothes or not. Women may wish to dress to look attractive. This does not ever mean that they are 'asking' to be raped or that they deliberately set out to provoke a sexual assault. No woman wants to be or asks to be raped. That is a contradiction in terms.

'The woman must have led him on. It must be her fault.'

A woman's body is her own. She has a right to engage in any sexual contact she chooses, and to disengage from it when and how she chooses. She has a right to say 'No' and be believed and to be treated with respect.

'If you fight back you make things worse for yourself.'

There is no evidence to support this. Many women who have fought back have escaped much worse injury by doing so. A man with a knife may say that a woman will be all right if she does what he says. Unfortunately he often fails to keep his word and the woman is injured anyway. Only the woman in each situation can decide whether she is safer if she fights back.

It *is* possible to escape from an intended rape. One of the problems is that the 'unsuccessful' rapes are not reported, while some sections of the press appear almost to glory in the details of vicious rapes and murders. Thus, the idea survives that a rapist can always have his own way through terrorising his victims.

Defending yourself

In attempted rape, as with other kinds of assault, there is no 'right' or 'wrong' way to defend yourself. You must use your intuition to assess the situation at the time. Some tactics success-fully used by women have been:

● Distracting the attacker for a moment by the ancient trick of pretending to see someone behind him, pushing him away, then running off at top speed.

Where the attack is made by a complete stranger you might try:

● Asking him about himself and telling him about yourself so that he sees you as a human being, not an object.

● Reproaching him on human terms. For instance, one woman escaped from rape by an armed attacker by keeping on talking to him and saying over and over again 'You'll be so sorry you did this. I haven't hurt you, why do you want to hurt me?' The man eventually let her walk away physically unharmed.

● Pretending to agree to sex as a way of waiting for a better moment to escape. For instance, one woman was dragged into an alleyway by a total stranger, while she was on her way to collect her small daughter from her mother's house. When he had her on the ground, she said, 'Do you want to make love to me?' The man nodded. 'We might get into trouble if we stay here', she said. 'Let's go to my house – it's empty.' The man helped her up and picked up the library books he had scattered. Once out in the open again, the woman gave him a hefty push and ran off unharmed.

While this is often an excellent tactic, you have to remember that if an attacker does succeed in his rape, he might use your apparent compliance against you in court.

- Pretending that someone else is within earshot who might come looking for you. Any delaying tactic is useful.
- Shouting for help – 'I don't know this man, he's hurting me, please help', if out of doors. Indoors it has been said that a cry of 'Fire' will arouse more interest than 'Rape!' or 'Help!'
- A rape by someone you know is often preceded by 'sexy' conversation about your appearance or your marital status. Some women have been raped in these situations because they have been 'too embarrassed' to protest, or afraid of hurting the man's feelings. Your own feelings matter more than the feelings of someone with whom you do not wish to have a sexual relationship. You matter too much as a human being to be forced into sex you do not want.
- There is often a moment when a man is vulnerable – for instance, when he's taking his trousers down or trying to lever himself on top of you. You may be able to kick at, or twist his testicles. Hitting back, hard, like this *as long as you do it effectively* will temporarily disable your attacker immediately. He will be in no state to rape or harm you in any way for some time. You may find the thought of this utterly repellent. However, remember that it may be better to fight back than to suffer the indignity, physical hurt and humiliation of rape. You have defended yourself *because* you have been attacked:

> I was walking the dog one dark night along a country lane. Suddenly I felt strong arms wrap around me from behind, pinioning me. I knew the man couldn't immediately hurt me because his hands were too busy holding me, so I didn't waste time and energy struggling. He then moved around the front and grasped the waistband of my trousers, trying to pull them off. As soon as he let go of my arms I cracked him over the head with the heavy torch I'd been carrying. I can even now hear the scrunch of the skull! He immediately released me and ran off into the darkness.

Remember, you can bide your time, as this story shows, especially if your attacker cannot move because he is holding you. In fact, being held provides a good opportunity for you to calm down, breathe normally and plan your strategy. As soon as he starts to loosen his clothing (and therefore releases part of you), use the moment to your advantage to catch him by surprise and strike him effectively.

Fighting can be a real choice in attempted rape. It will give you confidence and skill if you work on the techniques shown in this book, particularly those described on these two pages and page 80. Remember that you can bide your time if necessary. Practise falling and wrestling. Get used to fighting on the floor so that you are not afraid of falling down.

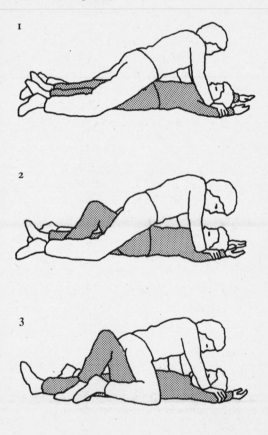

(1) The attacker is lying on top of you, holding your arms down. (2) Bend either knee up between his legs. (3) Firmly place the sole of your foot flat on the floor. (4) Keeping your foot firmly planted, push your hip on the side of the bent knee into the attacker. At the same time bring your hands down by your side to upset you attacker's balance. (5) Roll over powerfully to throw your attacker off you.

Each situation is different and every woman has to make her own choice whether or not to fight. Use your intuition to assess what is best. Sometimes your choice might indeed be between rape and death. In this situation you choose the way that will preserve your life. Some women faint while they are being raped because it is too much to bear. They block off the rape in order

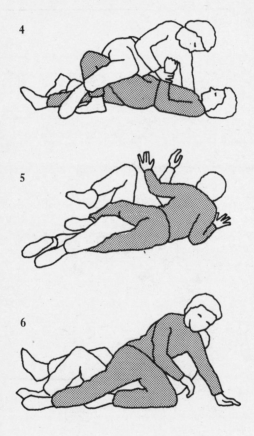

Your hips act as both a strong lever and as a support. This movement also breaks his grip on your hands. (6) Escape as quickly as possible. This technique and the one on page 80 require very little strength although they involve throwing your attacker off your body.

to survive and keep their sanity. In this way they protect some part of their minds and emotions. They may only gradually remember what happened as they recover enough to face what happened. They may never remember. It is important to value this form of self-protection as much as any other. In the end, only you can decide what the risks are and make a positive choice of what to do.

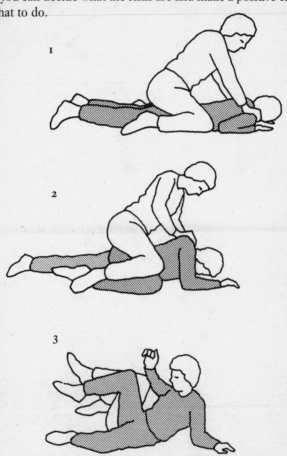

(1) The attacker is sitting on your back, holding your shoulders down. (2) Slide either knee up and tuck it into your body as closely as possible. (3) Using your knee on the floor as a lever, roll over powerfully to throw your attacker off you. Escape as quickly as possible.

What to do if you have been raped

Go to someone you trust. You may want to talk. Alternatively you may simply need to feel safe and to be looked after. You may need to rage, cry, or withdraw. There are no 'right' reactions. Your reaction is the one you need in order to preserve yourself.

Rape brings up strong feelings in all of us – feelings of rage, helplessness, guilt and shame. You may find that the person you confide in cannot listen to you carefully without making judgements. If this happens, try to ask clearly for the support you need. This may be one way of starting to feel in control again after the powerlessness of being raped.

If you don't feel you are being helped, contact your nearest Rape Crisis Centre (see page 110). This is run by women who are trained to counsel women who have been raped or sexually assaulted. They will always believe you. They aim to offer support and information without making judgements or putting pressure on you to take one course rather than another.

Although you may wish to report the rape to the police you are under no obligation to do so. If you do decide to go to the police you will have to follow their procedures. For instance, you will have to have a medical examination and make a statement. If you go to Rape Crisis or the Samaritans, they will put your needs first and offer you counselling and support. They will also explain in more detail what you will have to do at the police station and so help you to see more clearly what your choices are.

If you do report the rape, remind yourself constantly that you have a right to justice. A man has raped you. You have the right to see that he does not get away with it. Police practice is to question you at length and to make you go over your story several times, because they want to get it straight. This will be difficult because you have just been through a terrifying experience. You may well be confused, angry and upset. However, the police need a clear statement in order to press charges. Remember that you have a right to justice, care and respect. In the long term it may help to remind yourself that although you have been a victim of rape, you are also a rape survivor.

Whether or not you decide to report the rape, it is important to seek medical help. You will need tests to ascertain that you have not contracted VD or become pregnant as a result of the rape.

Contacting the police

If you do decide to involve the police, it is important to act quickly. Many women feel that they are far too upset at the time to talk to the police, but in fact you are less likely to be believed if you allow several days to elapse. Similarly, it is very important not to destroy any possible medical evidence by bathing, washing yourself or changing and washing your clothing, however much you want to. You may also feel that an alcoholic drink or a tranquilliser would help you. However, it is important not to take drink or drugs as you need to be able to tell your story coherently.

Ask a friend or member of your family to go with you to the police station. If there is no one you feel you can ask, your local Rape Crisis Centre should be able to send someone to be with you.

The police will ask a doctor to examine you both internally and externally. You can ask for your own GP or a woman doctor to do this. The doctor will be looking for evidence which will establish the rape.

You are likely to be asked to tell your story many times, and you must expect to be asked extremely personal questions. Eventually a police officer will take down a written statement based on your account of what happened. You will be given time to read it. If it does not represent what you feel occurred, you can ask for the statement to be changed. It is now normal practice for a woman police officer to be present. If you find that the officers you deal with are all men, you can ask to deal with a woman. If you are unhappy about the way you are being treated, you can ask to see someone more senior.

It may be important for you to know that if your case does come to court, your anonymity can be guaranteed. Even at the time of your first interview you can ask for it to be noted that you do not want your name mentioned in court.

Defending yourself against weapons

An armed attacker is clearly extremely dangerous and you have to think very carefully about your possible reactions. He may be carrying a stick, a broken bottle, a club or a knife.

It is important to know that not all attacks with knives end in rape or murder. This means there is proof that it is possible to protect yourself and that you can still make choices even in dangerous situations. In this section we talk mainly about knives, but the same principles apply to other weapons:

I was walking out in the country when a young man jumped out at me and held a knife to my throat. He said the most terrible things about what he was going to do to me. Just then, quite by chance, a police car went by in the distance with its siren going. The boy turned his head to listen and as he did so I reached up and took the knife away from him. I was so angry with him that I gave him a real telling off. I said: 'What would your family think of you if they knew you did this sort of thing? You ought to be ashamed of yourself'. He was quite frightened of me by then. So I thought the best thing to do was to give him back his knife and send him on his way which I did. I was very shaken and upset afterwards, especially as I was on a course and none of the people in charge took it seriously and I didn't want to make a fuss. But at the time I thought: 'How dare he do this to me?' and I got very angry.

I was on my way home and a man with a knife appeared and said he was going to drag me into the bushes and rape me. I really stood my ground and I started to tell him everything about me. I told him about my job and my family . . . all kinds of things. I wanted to show him that I was ME, with my own life, that I wasn't just an object for him to do whatever he wanted to. In the end I said: 'Well, it's been nice talking to you' and I walked away. I think I must have surprised him by not acting the way he expected me to.

> I was alone at a reception desk when a boy walked in off the streets and flicked open his knife close to my face. I didn't think, I just said: 'Wow, that's a nice knife. Where did you get it?' He closed up the knife, put it back in his pocket and walked away again. I don't think he knew what to do.

All these women used their intuition and their sense of being a valuable person to forestall their attackers. It might be hard for you to imagine being strong in these situations. The images we see on television and the stories we read in the newspapers tend to reinforce the idea that an attacker with a knife is all-powerful. Probably none of these three stories would be considered 'newsworthy' because the women involved were not hurt or killed. Such stories are rarely reported.

Before we look at simple physical techniques for dealing with attacks with knives, here are some points to remember when practising.

1 Practising self-defence against this sort of attack can be particularly disturbing because knives evoke such strong fears in most people. This can be reinforced by press reports which appear to glory in the details of savage attacks. So it is important to practise slowly and to take time to talk about those fears. Part of self-defence is being able to look more steadily at your fear, to share it with others and to try to understand it together. This is a way to start changing fear into something that can give power and strength. Sharing feelings breaks down isolation. The frightening images are then no longer a private secret, too powerful even to mention out loud. For some people it is important to know that their fears are real, that they are not silly and that other people feel the same way.

2 It can easily seem as though the knife has a power of its own. Remember that it is only as dangerous as the person holding it and that you can talk to an attacker with a knife, as with any other attack. So make sure that you know where the knife is at all times, but address the person behind it. It is easy to see the man with a knife as a robot or monster. Remember that he is a human being. He too can feel shame or guilt, embarrassment or fear. You may be able to find a way to appeal to something in him in the same way as with any other attack.

3 Think about how you use knives skilfully and with little thought in ordinary situations such as cooking. You may also

have taken a knife from someone else quite safely when you needed to – because you were in a hurry or because you saw a child using it dangerously. You do know how to handle knives.

4 Some attackers carry knives for bravado. Others may pick up a knife or another weapon because it is lying near at the time. Some expect to use it; others hope not to but might if they panic. Any knife attack should be taken seriously – assume your attacker *is* prepared to use the knife and at the same time look for ways to prevent him from doing so. Try to remember to put knives away at home so that they are not easily available as weapons to intruders.

5 If you are attacked, try to put some furniture between you and the attacker. Perhaps you could grab a chair and use it to keep him at a distance. You might protect your arm with a cloth or clothing if you go to grab his wrist and take control of the knife. It is important to think about what would be available to you as protection in different situations as in a struggle your attacker could easily cut you with his knife.

6 In a real attack you would have to use your intuition to help you assess the situation. It is still possible to make choices however dangerous it may seem. Remember that you can bide your time until there is a real opportunity for you to fight back or take control of the situation. If you are forced to make a bargain about your safety – to give your attacker what he wants so that he will not hurt you – bear in mind that he may not keep to his side of the bargain. You certainly do not have to keep to your side if you can see another way out.

7 When you practise, work slowly and carefully. You can start by noticing how you use knives in ordinary situations and gradually work towards practising against a proper attack. Leave time to talk as you practise, and time to wind down at the end.

8 Find out by experimentation how to loosen a grip. Always aim to get firm control of the wrist and arm first so that you control the hand holding the knife. You can start by sitting down next to a partner with one of you lightly holding a pencil. Work out how to twist the wrist and open the grip. At this stage it might feel safer to deal with all the different factors of a knife attack separately. So practise disarming someone in slow careful stages.

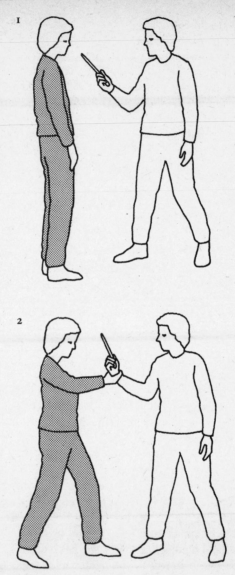

(1) You are confronted by an attacker with a knife or club. (2) Firmly grasp the attacker's wrist so that you can control its movement. At the same time move out of the path of the knife. (3) Push the knife edge of your other hand into the crook of the attacker's elbow, still holding the wrist tightly. (4) Force his forearm

3

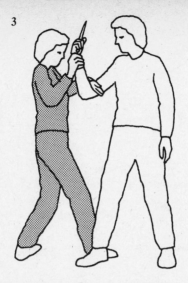

4

back and down to the outside of his upper arm. This movement twists the shoulder and elbow joints against themselves, forcing him to open his grip and drop the weapon.

Attacks on children

The possibility that your child may be attacked is an ever-present worry for any parent. At the same time it is hard to talk to children about it, or to prepare them to deal with it. You may find it embarrassing to talk about the generally sexual nature of these attacks.

The most common approaches made to children by strangers in the lead-up to an attack are:
- offering the child sweets
- persuading the child to go for a ride in a car; suggesting a trip to a funfair or a beach
- asking for directions, then suggesting the child gets in the car to show the way in person
- saying there are puppies or kittens 'at home' which the child might like to see
- pretending to be a policeman who wants the child's help in searching for a criminal
- pretending to be sent by a hospital because the child's parents have had an accident

A child-attacker will usually be a man, but it may be a couple or a woman on her own.

However, many sexual attacks on children are carried out by people already known to the child. They may be friends of the family, a teacher, a doctor, or a house parent in a children's home. They may be a member of the family. They may, like the stranger, offer treats to win the child's trust. What they all have in common is that they have authority over the child. They are people for whom the child is expected to feel love or respect. They are far more likely to be believed should the child tell anyone what has happened.

This question of adults' authority over children is a central and paradoxical problem in preparing children to cope with an attack. We bring children up to be respectful to adults and people in authority. Yet a child who encounters an attacker must somehow override that authority. The child must be ready to be rude and disobedient. We train children to say 'thank you' and accept politely when offered a present or a treat, yet we must also expect them to know how to refuse an attacker's bribe.

What should we tell them?

Recently on a bus a man was playing and making friends with a small girl sitting on the seat in front with her mother. As he got off he tried to give the girl some sweets. He was most offended when her mother refused, saying she did not want her daughter to accept gifts from strangers. Think how much harder it would be for a child alone to refuse such an offer, wanting the sweets, and also afraid of being rude. Tell your children that they may have to be rude in such encounters and that you will not be angry with them if they are.

Most attacks by adults on children are sexual. It is important to find a straightforward way to talk about this, because veiled comments about men who do 'horrible things to you' conjure up confusing images, and make it difficult for a child to know when something happens whether this is what they have been warned about:

> My mum used to tell me vague stories about 'strange men doing nasty things'. I knew she meant sex even though I barely knew what sex was. I also knew that sex was something she did with my dad. If it was nasty why did they do it? *And anyway what was it?* Now I feel she could have talked to me about sex between two willing people and how that is different from being forced. No-one likes to be forced to do anything they don't want to, even if it is something they normally enjoy. Children understand that only too well!

When you introduce the possibility of sexual encounters also talk about what to do: ignoring or laughing at a 'flasher', telling the adult to stop; pretending a parent is in earshot even if they are not; recruiting help from other people ... many of the other tactics suggested in this book for adults can also be used by children.

In general, whenever you talk about the different ploys the attacker might use, and the different things he might do, discuss the various ways the child might deal with them – for instance, refusing politely, refusing abruptly, pretending not to hear, threatening to take a car number, checking the adult's identity with other adults, and so on.

It will help, too, to talk in general terms about who the attacker might be and to introduce the possibility that it might be some-one they know: 'some children are attacked by relations or teachers, or friends of their parents . . .' In that way you allow for the possibility without suggesting that they be frightened of specific people.

Children often want to talk several times about their worries. You may find this difficult, especially if they want to talk about painful and frightening events, involving possible violence and attack. Try to overcome your reluctance. They are doing it because they need to be clear, to understand the dangers. Chil-dren are more frightened by vague possibilities than by the truth. Share your doubts and fears but don't let them become too over-whelming. It is good for them to see that you can not only be frightened but also overcome those fears.

Two general precautions may be sensible. First, you can train your children to make a point of telling you first if they are going somewhere, for instance, to buy an ice lolly or visit a friend. With younger children this is difficult because they are impulsive and have short memories. Older children, say over six or seven, should be capable of remembering. Explaining the reason for the rule will make it easier for them to accept it.

Many children enjoy the fun of wearing T-shirts on which their own names have been printed. It is probably better to keep these for occasions when children are safely under your super-vision. A potential attacker who appears to know a child's name may be more persuasive and therefore more dangerous. Similarly, try to avoid the type of school satchel which has a clear plastic window on the outside where the child's name and address may be easily read at a distance. If your child does have this type of satchel, put his or her name and address inside and leave the label blank.

It is important to discuss the different possibilities for resist-ance with children. Let them find, through talking and practising, which techniques they feel they could and could not do, and let them think of their own ideas and strategies. Children have the great advantage of suppleness. Many children have escaped an attacker by wriggling determinedly and shouting for help. Another possibility is for them to sink to the floor and make themselves 'heavy'. Their age, size, strength and so on will affect which techniques they choose. But whatever their size and age, in an attack they will have to use their own resourcefulness and imagination. They can start developing and trusting that now.

How can you encourage these qualities?
● Develop resourcefulness through play, craft activities, letting children pay their own bus fares, do shopping, make telephone calls. In general, let them work out their own answers to problems.
● Give them real responsibilities appropriate to their age – for instance, making their own bed or washing up.
● Encourage physical competence, for instance, through games and sport or completing fiddly jobs. Be patient with a slow and clumsy child.
● When you refuse permission, explain why. Let them make their own choices as much as you can and let them take the consequences. A child with this experience is less likely to be persuaded by an attacker to do something dangerous or unpleasant.
● Build up confidence and self-respect by putting the emphasis on praise for achievements rather then criticism for mistakes. Show your respect and love for them so that they love and respect themselves.

On the next two pages we have written some advice specially for children to read for themselves. Or, if your children are too young, you could read it to them.

Advice for children to read

If you are worried about being attacked, find someone you can trust to discuss your worries. This may be your parents, another relative, a teacher or a friend.

Practise the techniques shown in this book with other children and with an adult who wants to help. Be careful not to practise with anyone who enjoys frightening you or making you feel silly. See which techniques work for you and change them if you can find ways that work better. Think about how you would get rid of or fight off someone bigger if you had to.

Practise different ways of saying 'no' and refusing co-operation with someone who is trying to make you do something that you don't want to do. You can practise with friends or with an adult. Whoever is playing the attacker should try different ways to persuade you – they could be friendly or pretend that your parents had sent them; they could bully you; they could pretend to be a social worker; they could pretend to be someone you know or a stranger. You should try different ways of refusing and getting away.

An attacker may be someone you know – a relative, a teacher, a friend of the family – or he may be a stranger. Usually it will be a man, but it may be a women, or a couple. This doesn't mean that you have to be frightened of everyone! Most of the people you know well would never try to hurt you.

If someone you know does do something you find strange or upsetting, that will affect how much you like and trust them. It may make you want to talk to them about it, or to keep out of their way, or to ask someone to help you to make sure it doesn't happen again.

If a stranger makes you feel upset or in danger, trust that feeling and get away as quickly as possible.

Think about how you might embarrass the attacker by laughing or shouting. Think about other adults you might ask for help and how you would speak to them.

Here are some of the ways an attack might happen and some ideas for coping with it:

● A stranger might say he has been sent by your mother (or someone else you know) to collect you from school or to take you somewhere. Or he may say that something has happened to your mother and that he will take you to the hospital.

Ask for information to see whether he really knows your mother – what does your mother look like? What is her name? If he can't answer then he is lying. If he can answer but you still feel uneasy about going with him – don't go. Run away, or explain to another adult nearby that you are frightened of this man and want to be left alone. You can ask an adult nearby to telephone your mother to find out if she sent someone in her place.

● A stranger may ask you to go in his car to show him the way somewhere. Don't go. Say you don't know the way even if you do. ALWAYS keep a good distance away from the car so that you can't be grabbed.

● A stranger or someone you know may try to touch your body and between your legs. If it is someone you know, they may do it when they are pretending to give you a 'friendly' hug. It may hurt, or it may feel uncomfortable. If you don't like the way someone touches you, think about the best way to stop them doing it. Could you ask him not to do it? Could you tell your mother or someone else you trust and ask them to talk to him? Could you just avoid being hugged by this person?

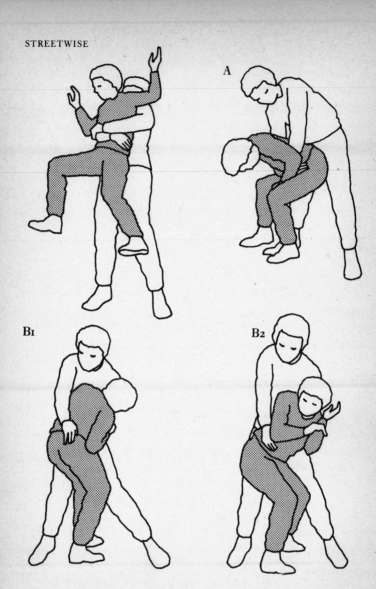

If someone picks you up and you want them to let go, (A) make yourself
floppy and heavy. Sink to the floor like a stone. When you are close to
the floor, slip through their arms and run away. (B) You can break
their grip by wriggling and twisting, making yourself slippery and
squirmy like an eel. You can also shout, kick and hit out until you are
free. Then run away. REMEMBER: Put all your strength and energy
into the escapes.

Incest

Incest is still a taboo subject. So, too, to a large extent, is sexual abuse of children by other adults who are generally respected and trusted by the child's family or the community, and so many of the problems are the same in both cases.

Official statistics suggest that incest happens only rarely. But recent surveys indicate that it may actually be far more widespread. Work with incest survivors shows how difficult it is to report the abuse. A girl who does report it is often threatened with further abuse and is generally disbelieved or blamed. It is rare for her to receive help.

With incest the first step can be the hardest. This is to admit that it is actually happening. People do not want to believe that someone they know, maybe someone they love, can do such a terrible thing. They cannot bear the consequences of acknowledging it and taking action. So it can often seem less immediately painful for the family as a whole to deny it, or to say that the child is making it up, or that she is provoking it, or that she enjoys the sexual experience, or that she is wicked.

Accepting any of these explanations allows the incest to continue. It leaves the child trapped in a situation from which she does not have the power or control to escape. And it leaves the blame for what is happening with her. If we are ever to recognise incest and be able to stop it and the severe damage it is doing, we must accept that it exists. People must be prepared to believe a child who says that incest is happening. Again, at worst, you may feel in the end that you have been foolish. More likely you may help a child escape regular sexual abuse from someone for whom she is expected to feel love and respect.

If your child has been attacked

Children who have been attacked or sexually assaulted, need to be encouraged to talk and be believed. They will be confused, frightened and possibly in pain. They may not have the language to describe what has happened, especially if they have never talked much about sex, or their bodies. They may hardly know themselves what has happened, only that they have been hurt and upset. They may have been sworn to secrecy, threatened with punishment, or told that you will be angry if you find out.

They bring a heavy burden to you and need all possible comfort and encouragement. Above all they need to be believed. When children feel they can trust you to deal fairly with them, you will gradually find out what has happened. Children who are frightened and made to feel guilty are likely to withdraw or become more and more confused.

Take time to decide on the best course of action. Try to find out what the child wants and needs. This is one way of giving back a sense of control after the experience of being powerless in an attack.

Consult your own feelings. You may well feel rage, helplessness and guilt, and want to *do* something, anything. Those feelings are natural. You, too, are hurt if your child is hurt. But taking care of yourself is a separate need from doing what is best for the child.

One woman who was sexually assaulted as a child by a friend of the family said 'I liked the man who did it, but I didn't want him to do that. He didn't hurt me physically, but I felt uncomfortable and wanted to tell him not to do it again. My parents were shocked and angry and rushed me off to the police station. The more they made me tell what he had done, the more ashamed I felt. And I was terrified of getting him into trouble. I was never allowed to see him again.'

Being attacked makes anyone, but especially a child, feel powerless. It is important to give them back some of the control by listening to their feelings about what has happened.

It is difficult for parents to know whether or not to involve the police. In a serious assault it is obvious that you must seek police help to protect other children. Many parents hesitate over contacting the police for minor offences. They may think that the child might be much more upset at police questioning or a court appearance than he or she was after the original offence. As with alleged rape, it may also be the case that children are not believed. This can have devastating consequences for their self-esteem. You can, however, report the crime to the police, without them questioning your child.

Perhaps the first thing, after comforting the child, is to consult a trusted friend, relative or someone with experience of dealing with child abuse. Remember that the police and social services have certain statutory duties and they may act without consulting you or the child. Voluntary agencies (see page 110) can provide someone to listen, to support you, and will also give you information on the legal position.

- Don't assume familiarity with children you don't know. You may feel that you know a child because you know his or her parents. But children tend not to feel they know you until they have had some proper contact.
- Don't be annoyed with children who are not immediately friendly; *you* may know that you mean no harm, but *they* cannot be sure.
- Respect children's physical dignity – don't pick them up and hug them just because you want to.
- Don't offer sweets, money or treats of any sort to children to whom you are a stranger.

Adults generally can take some responsibility for not frightening or confusing children. Remember that children are more vulnerable than adults because they are smaller and less powerful.

Help from other people

Sometimes you may need to obtain help from other people, whether it is a street attack or an incident in your own home.

Unfortunately you cannot always rely on passers-by to help you. They may be afraid of injury themselves, they may be unsure of whether it is a real struggle or just 'horsing around'. More commonly people may think that they just don't want to become involved.

Calling out

Try to think clearly of things you can do to make people certain that you want help.

> I was waiting at a bus stop when a man came up and put his arm round me and tried to pull me towards him. I struggled and shouted but he was very strong, and by this time had both his arms pinioning mine. There were two people watching, a man and a woman. I could see their uncertainty about whether I knew him or not. I shouted, 'He's a total stranger! He's hurting me, please help!' At the same time I stamped hard on one of his feet – I was wearing high heels at the time. Simultaneously the two people came forward to help and the man ran off, limping and shouting furious awful things at me.

Remember that it is far better to be embarrassed than to be hurt. It often works well to shout something specific. Shout 'My bag's been stolen' or 'Help, I'm being hurt'; that way, people around will know what is happening, and be more inclined to act. You could also ask specific people to help – 'Please – you in the blue coat . . .' so that it is harder for people to rush by.

Shout, scream and make as much noise as you can, so that people cannot ignore you easily.

Intervention

Alternatively, the roles may be reversed. You may be the passer-by and see someone else being attacked, and you may find yourself using similar excuses for not interfering: 'It's a husband and wife squabble', 'rights and wrongs on both sides', 'may make it worse to intervene', and so on.

These reasons do not stand up to logical analysis. Even if the two people do know each other, this does not make it all right for one of them to be seriously hurt by the other. Domestic disputes will not be resolved by violence. It is perfectly possible that a fight could get worse, but intervention may at least cool it down in the short term.

If you don't feel you can intervene physically there are many other possibilities. Remember it could be you being attacked and everyone else walking by.

● You could flag down a bus, or car to get help.
● You could stop other passers-by and recruit them to help.
● You could shout and scream to attract attention.
● You could ask the person being attacked if they wanted any help.
● You could order the attacker to stop.
● You could stand nearby, staring at him, and try to shame him into stopping.
● You could intervene by pulling the attacker off, and if necessary restraining both people from hitting each other further.

Obviously you will have to take all the circumstances into account, including your own strength and resources, and what help might be available quickly.

It is not easy to intervene in an attack, but if someone is getting hurt, always *do* something – even if it's only rushing off to call the police without anyone seeing you. Don't feel that you have to be heroic. We all have our limitations and we need to be realistic about what it is possible to do. Often, surprisingly little is required.

> I was waiting for a train in a tube station quite early one evening. It was relatively empty. I suddenly noticed a young woman with a man hanging round her. She looked embarrassed. I heard her hiss 'Please go away', but he didn't. She went and sat on a bench but he came and sat there too. She looked furious and worried. I didn't know whether they were boy and girlfriend having a row, or whether he was just a

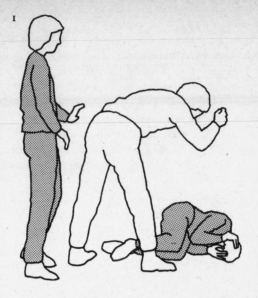

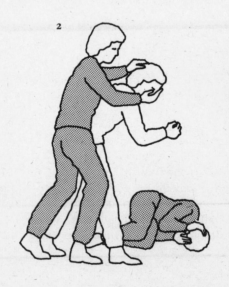

(1) You see someone being attacked. (2) From behind, put one hand under the attacker's chin and the other on the back of his head. You can also grasp a handful of his hair to get a better grip. (3) Pull the attacker backwards by

3

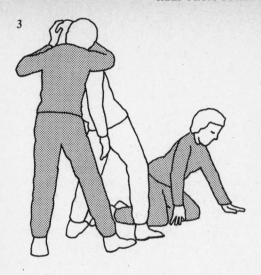

4

pushing up under his chin, holding the back of the head firmly with the other hand. (4) This gives the other person a chance to escape. If you continue to pull the attacker backwards he will overbalance and fall, allowing you to leave also.

nuisance. I came over to the bench and very deliberately sat close to the girl. The bloke immediately got up and disappeared down a 'No exit' route.

I asked her if he'd been bothering her, and she said he'd been following her for about 15 minutes. The simple act of another woman coming and sitting next to her was enough to get rid of him immediately.

Calling the police

You may need to call the police to obtain help for yourself, or because you have seen someone else being attacked.

It is good practice to keep the number of your local police station near your telephone where you can find it quickly without having to search a directory first. This is the number you should ring for help if it is not urgent. For instance, you may be worried because you have not seen your elderly neighbour for a few days, and cannot raise a reply from her door.

However, in an emergency where speed is essential, you should have no hesitation in ringing 999, either from your own home or from a callbox. 999 calls go straight to mobile police cars, so the response is rapid. Calls to the local police station may be filtered through several officers before anyone is able to come. You do not need money for a 999 call.

Panic is the main problem in using the 999 service. In their alarm and confusion many people fail to dial the number correctly. Remember that 9 is the *last but one* number on the dial. It is better to dial slowly and correctly, than to rush and make a mistake. Every minute can matter.

When the operator answers, you should immediately give your name and the telephone number where you are. Don't waste time describing what is happening at this stage. The operator will ask you which service you want: police, fire or ambulance. When the named service answers you should, once again, immediately give your name, the telephone number and where you are. Public call boxes always have an address on the instrument for just this purpose.

Try to describe briefly what you have seen, in enough accurate detail to help the emergency service decide what to do. For instance, saying 'There's a fire' and putting the telephone down does not help the fire service assess how many appliances to send

– it could be a fire in a rubbish bin or a whole house in flames.

Similarly, if someone is seriously injured, it helps if you can describe their injury. That way the ambulance service may be able to bring some special equipment which could save a life. Give the sex and age of the victim if you can. Where a woman has been attacked the police may want to send a woman police officer. It is important, too, to mention any weapons you have seen used: for instance, in an armed raid, the police may also need to be armed.

The emergency service operators are trained to help you give the appropriate information. Obviously, though, it saves vital minutes if you are already prepared to give your account succinctly and calmly.

When you have witnessed a crime, the police will want you to describe what you have seen and possibly to make a statement. It will help you to do this satisfactorily if you have trained yourself to be an accurate observer. Otherwise, it is surprising how quickly the details of a person's height, colouring and clothing will simply melt away in your mind. A good description will help the police enormously. You can practise improving your powers of observation in a bus or tube. Look at other passengers briefly then look away, and see how many you can describe to yourself. Car registration numbers are also often important in catching offenders. If you see a car in dubious circumstances, make a note of its number – it could be important evidence.

Many people feel reluctant to ring the police with a vague feeling that something is wrong: for instance, a 'housepainter' who is acting oddly, a smooth-talking caller who seems a little too keen to get into their house 'to use the 'phone . . .' Act on your intuitions – don't delay. Don't think 'Oh well, the police are very busy, I don't want to bother them', or 'I expect someone else will have rung'. Don't hesitate to call the police if you feel that it is the best way to deal with the problem.

A man knocked at the door of an elderly woman's house asking if she was 'a widow with a son', because the 'son' had broken down in his car and needed money for repairs. She was suspicious but sent him down the road to a friend who was equally doubtful about his story. Together they rang the police, and a con man who had plagued their district for weeks was caught in the act.

A sharp-eyed woman ticket collector was instrumental in trapping an armed rapist who had brutally attacked four women at her station. She saw him hanging around the station and recognised him as someone who had bought a ticket from her on the day of the last rape. Her excellent description provided the critical photofit picture of the rapist. He was caught and sent to prison.

A sympathetic ear

It is important to realise that the best self-defence in the world will not protect you against every single attack and help you cope with all eventualities. Defending yourself may still mean that you are hurt physically, even if you managed to get rid of your attacker.

Even if you have not suffered any physical harm, you may still experience shock and loss of confidence. You may need to cry, shout and hit out. You may need to talk and talk, telling and retelling your story to sympathetic friends and family. See if you can find ways to think positively about the experience. For instance, there may be aspects of what you did which saved you from more serious injury. Try to explain to the people around you what you need and how they can help you. They may also feel angry and upset at what has happened. Sometimes in this situation people may put pressure on you to 'get over it' quickly, because they cannot cope with your grief and hurt. In such cases, it would be better to go elsewhere for help if necessary.

What ever happens, remember that it was not your fault that you were attacked. You did not ask for it, nor did you 'deserve' it.

The law and self-defence

In some countries it is perfectly legal to carry guns, knives or sprays for possible use in defending yourself. In Britain this is not so. The law severely restricts the amount of force that can be used and the 'weapons' that may be carried.

When can you defend yourself?

The law allows you to defend your family and your property, but the reason for defending yourself must be lawful.

If you do have to defend yourself, you can only use *as much force as is necessary*. Once the situation is under control, you must stop. You could find yourself prosecuted for assault or grievous bodily harm if you hit back with more force than has been used on you.

There are no set answers about how much force you can use to defend yourself. It depends on all the circumstances at the time. However, the basic guideline is that 'reasonable' force can be used, but no more. If someone attacks you and you get him down on the ground, then run away, that is self-defence. But if you follow this up by kicking him gratuitously, that is excessive force.

What weapons can you carry?

The law discourages carrying weapons for self-defence. In law almost anything could be construed as a 'weapon' depending on the circumstances.

Some books and articles on self-defence have encouraged people to carry rolled-up magazines, pepper or hair spray. Any or all of these could in fact be construed as an 'offensive weapon', and you could find yourself in trouble if challenged by the police. The basic rule is that if you have something in a street or public place made or adapted as a weapon and intended to be used as a weapon, then that is a possible offence.

On the other hand, materials or objects carried 'on reasonable excuse' or 'lawful authority' would be acceptable. For instance, pepper would probably not be considered a weapon if you had just bought it and could produce a receipt. A pointed steel comb or long, sharp scissors would probably not be regarded as a weapon if you could prove you were a hairdresser on your way to work at the time of the attack on you. However, pepper, sharp combs or scissors might be classified as weapons if they were discovered in your bag or pocket at a party.

Flick knives and gravity knives are always considered offensive weapons and prohibited in law. CS gas or chemical mace sprays are prohibited under the Firearms Act. If you are found carrying any of these you are liable to a heavy sentence.

Just as important as the legal considerations is the likely reality of using a weapon. You may be carrying something which is not actually a weapon but could be used as such in an emergency. It may give you confidence to know that you have it. But could you actually get at it quickly enough in a sudden confrontation? Always remember, too, that if you do take out a weapon in self-defence *it could be used against you.* Your attacker may be more used to weapons than you, and he may well be stronger. In a serious confrontation weapons are not carefully aimed, they are used quickly, desperately and probably inefficiently. If you take out a penknife, a bunch of keys or a comb to defend yourself you are unlikely to be practised in its use as a weapon. The most likely course of events is that your attacker would seize your 'weapon' and use it on you.

However, many people have successfully defended themselves with the everyday objects they were carrying in less serious situations.

A young man tried to seize my shopping bag. He didn't know that, by chance, it had a pyrex casserole in it! I swung it at him. It thwacked him on the hand and he ran off, cursing.

Coming home one evening two teenagers came up one each side of me and tried to take my handbag. It had been a wet day so I had my umbrella. I used it like a fencing sword and jabbed at them. They said: 'Hey, it was only a joke, give us a chance, miss', and disappeared.

I still prefer the old-fashioned stiff bag to a modern soft one. Once, in Italy, a man pinched my bottom several times. It really hurt me. I boxed his ears with my bag . . . I hope he'll think twice about doing it again.

My keys were in my hand ready to get into my car when someone grabbed my wrist. I gouged the key down his arm and he let go. I drove off safely.

Summing up, there are two considerations which really matter. First, is what you are carrying legal? Secondly, could it be taken from you and used against you?

Personal alarms

Alarms can be useful as long as you do not rely on them as your sole means of self-defence. Personal alarms vary in size, price and weight, but basically they look something like a pocket torch and make a loud shrieking noise when activated. The idea is that an attacker will be startled and, with luck, will run off through fear of someone coming to your aid. The unpleasantly loud noise that most alarms make is probably sufficient at least to rouse the curiosity of people who might open doors or windows to investigate what is going on.

Some alarms are activated by pressurised air, some are battery-powered. One type of alarm is operated by pressing a button; other designs have a 'pin', like a grenade, which starts the alarm when it is pulled out. Alarms can now be bought at most large deparment stores, or at hardware and specialist security shops.

Some people feel that the main value of personal alarms is that they give you a sense of confidence which is communicated in the way you walk. The very fact that you possess an alarm also shows that you have recognised the possibility of attack, therefore you are more alert and less likely to be a victim.

Critics of alarms have pointed out that people sometimes keep their alarms in inaccessible places – for instance, at the bottom of a handbag – and that the noise often does not continue long enough to summon help. Also, the same objection can be made to personal alarms as to burglar alarms on houses: will anyone actually take any notice?

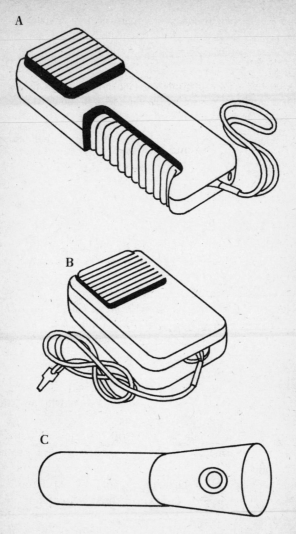

You can activate these personal alarms by: (A) squeezing them; (B) pulling out a 'pin' like a grenade; or (C) pressing and holding down the top.

The most practically designed alarms will have some or all of these features:

● the noise continues even if your thumb is not pressed down on the trigger. Having to keep your finger on the trigger will pre-occupy you and may prevent you fighting back in the most approriate ways. The alarm might also be snatched from you, so it is important for it to go on shrieking.

● the noise must be loud and truly objectionable.

● the noise should continue for at least thirty seconds and the power unit should last a reasonable length of time.

● ideally the alarm should give some indication if the power is running down. A battery-powered alarm which also has a light will indicate whether the battery is working or not.

However, you must choose the device which you feel suits you best. Look at and try out a range before making your selection.

A newer device is the 'anti-rape phial' which can be pinned to the underside of a lapel. Its virtue is that if it is broken it releases an obnoxious smell which may surprise and deter an attacker. The smell clings to his clothes so may also make him easier to identify. The phial is sold with an 'antidote' for your own clothes! The main objections are that it may be broken accident-ally, and secondly, as with alarms, that you may not be able to reach it quickly enough in an emergency.

A whistle is a cheap, alternative way of surprising an attacker, but again you have to ask yourself if you would have time to use it. Also, a whistle may not make enough noise to attract attention. The safest way to carry a whistle is attached to your clothes by a string and safety pin. It is better not to wear it round your neck.

Remember, though, that the best self-defence comes from inside – from how you feel about yourself. Possessing and carry-ing an alarm may increase your confidence, but it is not the total answer to every situation.

Useful addresses

Rape Crisis Centres

Aberdeen
PO Box 123, Aberdeen
Monday 6–8pm
Thursday 7–9pm
(0224) 575560

Belfast
PO Box 46, Belfast BT2 7AR
Tuesday to Friday 7–10pm
(0232) 249696

Birmingham
PO Box 558
Birmingham B3 2HL
(021) 233 2655
24-hr (021) 233 2122

Bradford
PO Box 155
Bradford BD5 7PW
Monday 1–5pm
Thursday 6–10pm
(0274) 308270

Brighton
PO Box 332, Hove, Sussex
Tuesday 6–9pm
Friday 3–9pm
Saturday 10am–1pm
(0273) 699756

Bristol
c/o The Women's Centre
44 The Grove, Bristol
Monday to Friday 10am–4pm
(0272) 22760

Cambridge
Box R, 12 Mill Road
Cambridge
Monday 7–9pm
Wednesday 6–12pm
Saturday 11am–5pm
(0223) 358314

Canterbury
PO Box 75, Canterbury
Every evening 6–9pm
(0227) 50400

Cardiff
Box 18, 108 Salisbury Road
Cathays, Cardiff
Monday 7–10pm
Wednesday 11am–2pm
Thursday 7–10pm
(0222) 373181

Cleveland
PO Box 31, Middlesborough
Cleveland TS4 2JJ
Thursday 7–10pm
(0642) 813397

Coventry
PO Box 176
Coventry CV1 2QS
Monday 11am–3pm, 7–10pm
Tuesday to Friday 7–10pm
(0203) 77229

Derby
Thursday 8–10pm
(0332) 372 545

Dublin
PO Box 1027, Dublin 6, Eire
Monday to Friday 8pm–8am
Saturday and Sunday 24hr
(0001) 601 470

Edinburgh
PO Box 120
Head Post Office
Edinburgh EH1 3ND
Monday, Wednesday, Friday
1–2pm, 6–8pm
Thursday 7–10pm
(031) 566 9437

Glasgow
PO Box 53, Glasgow G2 1YR
Monday, Wednesday, Friday
7–10pm
(041) 221 8448

Leeds
PO Box 27, Wellington St
Leeds LS2 7EG
Monday–Friday, 10am–5pm
(0532) 441323
Every day 10am–midnight
(0532) 440058

Leicester
Tuesday 7–10pm
Saturday 2–5pm
(0536) 666666

Liverpool
Monday 7–9pm
Thursday 2–5pm
Friday 6–8pm
Saturday 2–5pm
(051) 734 4369

Urgent messages at any other
time
(051) 427 2338

London
PO Box 69, London WC1 9NJ
Weekdays 10am–6pm
(01) 278 3956
24 hr (01) 837 1600

Manchester
PO Box 336
Manchester M60 2BS
Tuesday 2–5pm, Wednesday
6–9pm
Thursday 6–9pm, Friday
2–5pm
Sunday 6–9pm
(061) 228 3602

Norwich
Monday 7–10pm, Thursday
7–10pm
Friday 11am–2pm
(0603) 667687

Nottingham
c/o 37a Mansfield Road
Nottingham
Monday–Friday 11am–5pm
(0602) 410440

Oxford
Women's line
Wednesday 2–10pm
(0865) 726295

Portsmouth
Wednesday 7–10pm, Friday
7pm–7am

Portsmouth – *contd*
Saturday 7–10pm, Sunday
3–6pm
(0705) 669511

Reading
Box 9, 17 Chatham St,
Reading
Sunday 7.30–10 pm
(0734) 55577

Sheffield
PO Box 34, Sheffield
Monday 10am–1pm, 7–9pm
Tuesday 8–10pm
Wednesday 2–4pm
Friday 10am–1pm
Saturday 12–3pm
(0742) 755255

Tyneside
PO Box 13, Newcastle
Monday to Friday 10am–10pm
Saturday and Sunday
6.30–10pm
(0632) 329858

Citizens Advice Bureaux
Head Office
110 Drury Lane, London WC2
(01) 836 9231
Also check your local directory
for the nearest branch.

Samaritans
Head Office
17 Uxbridge Road
Slough, Berkshire SL1 1SN
Slough 32713
Also, check your local
directory for the branch
nearest you.

Self-defence classes
For information about self-
defence classes, we suggest
that you phone your local
authority and ask about Adult
Education classes in your area.
You can also phone your local
Women's Centre or Rape Crisis Centre for information
about all-women classes. Also,
see page 34 in this book.

Women's Aid Federation
Women's Aid Federation England
374 Gray's Inn Road
London WC1
(01) 837 9316   *and*
c/o Manchester Women's
Centre
116 Portland St, Manchester
(061) 228 1069

Welsh Women's Aid
Incentive House
Adam St, Cardiff
South Wales
(0222) 462291

Scottish Women's Aid
Ainslie House
11 St Colme St, Edinburgh
(031) 225 8011

Northern Ireland Women's Aid Federation
143a University Street
Belfast BP7 1HP
Northern Ireland
(0232) 249041 and 249358